Simple Healing Tools

ON THE PATH TO PERSONAL EMPOWERMENT
AND INNER PEACE

Carol Hansen Grey

Open Heart Press
Concord, CA

Published and distributed in the United States by:
Open Heart Press, P.O. Box 6722, Concord, CA 94524-1722
(925) 974-9088
www.openheartpress.com

Cover Design: Charles Ewers, Pinpoint Design (c-ewers@pacbell.net)
Cover Photographs and Interior Book Design: Carol Hansen Grey

ISBN 978-0-9658516-6-4

Library of Congress Catalog Card Number: 2009923519

FIRST EDITION
10 9 8 7 6 5 4 3 2 1

*This book is dedicated to all the teachers
in my life who have helped me
navigate this journey.*

ACKNOWLEDGMENTS

This book represents a lifetime journey and as such there are countless people to thank who have helped keep me on the path: family, friends, teachers and chance acquaintances who have shown up at just the right time to shine a light when I needed it most. To all of you, I thank you!

A special thank you goes to my beloved husband and life-partner, Victor Grey, without whose love, support and encouragement this book never would have been written. I also wish to thank my children who have always been lights in my life and my greatest teachers.

I am especially grateful to those who helped with the publishing of this book: Kris Landgraf, Emogene Yates, Megan David, Rhonda Hull and Susan Miller for their proofreading and editing skills; Judy Whitson and Jean Shinoda Bolen for their loving advice and support; and Charles Ewers for his graphic design skills in creating the cover and his advice on the book layout. Thank you!

CONTENTS

🍁 PART 1: THE STORIES 🍁

INTRODUCTION

*E*mbracing change can be a difficult and
challenging endeavor. We all know, however,
that change is inevitable — nothing is static.
Just as the cells in our bodies are in a continual state
of change, with every new thought, our minds change
and expand. With every new birth and every death, our
world changes. The universe itself is in a continual state
of growth and expansion. Because we all are part of
this ever changing universe, it serves us to pay attention
and to heed the call when it becomes apparent that we
need to make a change in our lives.

There will be early signs that begin to nudge us, gently
at first, to let us know it is time to make a change. It
may begin simply as an uncomfortable or restless feeling.
In those early stages, if we take the time to examine the
feeling, we can often make the needed shift without too
much disruption in our lives. However, if we ignore the
initial nudging, the signs become more apparent until we
have no choice but to pay attention.

Even though it may appear the signs are coming from
outside of us, the truth is they are coming from deep

within us to let us know it is time to grow beyond our perceived limitations. The longer we choose to ignore these inner promptings, the more uncomfortable our lives become until we finally pay attention and make the necessary change. I think of our response to these promptings as a transformational healing journey. My hope is you will find the stories within these pages, and the tools I share, to be of service to you on your own journey of personal transformation and healing.

I believe we are all spiritual beings and one of our primary goals as humans is to remember and awaken to our spiritual essence. This often entails undergoing a profound spiritual experience—some call it an awakening. In the pages of this book, I take you on my own transformational healing journey. It began in 1985 when I responded to a not so gentle inner nudge prompting me to make a major change in my life. I divorced my husband of twenty years and moved with my three children from our comfortable home in Wisconsin to the unfamiliar landscape of the San Francisco Bay Area.

This set the stage in the summer of 1991 for my transformational awakening. My oldest daughter, Kris, was living on her own in California and my fourteen-year-old son, Greg, had been living with his father in Indiana for two years. My twelve-year-old daughter, Liz, who was living at home with me, became the victim of a gang of girls who were threatening her on her way home from school every day. The school authorities told me they could do nothing since it didn't take place on school property. The police told me they could do nothing unless she was actually attacked. Thus, Liz was living

in a continual state of fear. In speaking with my ex-
husband about the situation, he suggested it might be
best if Liz came to live with him in Indiana. This idea
ripped open my heart — this was my baby! How could
I send her that far away? I told him this was not a decision I could make — it was a decision that only Liz could
make.

Liz really didn't know her father as we had separated
when she was three years old. However, after talking
it over with her, she decided that she wanted to give it
a try. So, in the summer of 1991, I flew with Liz to my
parents' home in Wisconsin. Her father drove from
Indiana to pick her up and take her back with him.

Words cannot fully describe the emotional upheaval
I was feeling. However, as I look back I realize the
Universe was working in wondrous ways. While in
Wisconsin I visited with a dear friend who gifted me
with a book, saying it had changed her life. I read it on
the plane trip back to California.

The book, *The World Beyond* by Ruth Montgomery,
was the first metaphysical book I had ever read. I found
it awakened in me a memory of when I was three years
old, telling my mother, "When I get born again, I want
to have you and daddy as parents again."

I remember my mom asking, "What do you mean when
you get born again?"

"You know," I responded, "when I get **born** again."

Mom looked at me and said, "Honey, people don't get born again. We all get born, we live our lives, and then we die and go to heaven."

I remember thinking, "How come she doesn't know that's not the way it works?" But, being only three, I wasn't equipped to have a philosophical conversation about reincarnation. So, it was never mentioned again and my Catholic upbringing definitely buried any idea of reincarnation. The thought laid dormant in my subconscious to be awakened 45 years later by Ruth Montgomery!!

I was so inspired by the ideas in the book that I bought all 10 books written by Ruth Montgomery. I also bought 10 copies of *A World Beyond* and sent them to friends and relatives in Wisconsin, hoping they would be as inspired by the book as I was. Upon receiving my gift, however, many of them actually became concerned for me, thinking that I might have joined a cult now that I was living alone in California without my kids!

I mark the reading of that book, however, as the beginning of my conscious spiritual awakening. In October of 1991, I was introduced to Reiki, a Japanese energy technique that promotes healing. The ability to use Reiki is transferred to the student during an attunement (or initiation process) given by a Reiki master. In October and December that year I received my first and second attunements. Within a year I had received all the attunements and became a Reiki Master-Teacher. I found that each attunement opened me more and more to my spiritual nature.

The simple, transformational and powerful tools I share with you in this book are those that I have discovered and used since that initial spiritual awakening. Over the years I have shared them with friends and clients, witnessing their healing power, and have come to believe that one of my purposes in this lifetime is to develop and share these simple healing tools with a wider audience. This book is a way for me to do that.

My belief is that planetary healing begins with each one of us taking the steps necessary to heal and empower ourselves. My hope is you will find within these pages, stories and processes helpful to you as you travel your own healing path to personal empowerment and inner peace.

HOW TO USE THIS BOOK

The book is divided into three parts:

* **Part 1** contains personal stories. These stories are in no particular order and often they overlap with one another. Feel free to skip around this section, reading the stories that call to you. The specific healing tools used in the stories are listed at the end of each story along with its chapter and page number to make it easy to reference them in Part 2.

* **Part 2** contains a detailed description of each healing tool mentioned in the stories as well as suggestions on how to use the tool. I created *Simple Healing Tools* in this way so the reader

could easily reference the tools without the need to go back through the stories to find a particular tool. All the tools can be found in Part 2.

✱ **Part 3** is a short list of resources I have found helpful along my path. Included are products, books and websites. A more extensive list of resources can be found on the SimpleHealingTools.com website where the list is continually expanded and updated.

Part 1

The Stories

a foggy Saturday morning and thought, "How perfect — even the outside sounds are muffled."

I went directly to my meditation room where I spent almost an hour in silent reflection. My usual practice would have included some reading or writing, but this was not permitted — just silence. I began to notice an uncomfortable feeling coming from deep within and settling around my shoulders.

Following my meditation I made breakfast and then embarked on the task of cleaning out my bookcases. Habit dictated I put on some music to provide a backdrop to any cleaning chore — but music was not allowed! Again I noticed an uncomfortable feeling tingling around my upper body. After about an hour of book sorting I realized, as I was taking books off the shelf, I was unconsciously opening them and reading passages.

STOP!! Reading is not allowed!

I then noticed my uncomfortable feeling had shifted into a feeling of being scared! My mind raced. How was I ever going to make it through the day? I felt like such a wimp! Anyone should be able to easily spend 24 hours in silence!

Of course, I knew it was not a life or death matter if I didn't accomplish the goal, but I was surprised at how difficult it actually was for me! I became even more determined to succeed and found as the day wore on, my mind quieted down making it easier to be in that silent space. I retired early in the evening (perhaps as an escape) looking forward to Sunday when I could resume my normal activities.

At our next spirituality class we discussed how we felt about the experience. It was comforting to learn that many other participants had also noticed feeling a sense of fear at the beginning of the process but after going through the fear, by the end of the day they felt a sense of peace. In exploring what might have brought on the fear, we came to a consensus that it was perhaps a fear of being alone. In the silence, however, we found we were able to connect at a deep level with Spirit. This connection brought with it a conscious certainty that we were not alone. Thus, the fear was transformed into a profound feeling of peace.

Although the exercise was not particularly pleasant for any of us, we all agreed it had been worthwhile. We each had learned something about ourselves and about the value of creating some silent times in our lives to connect more deeply with Spirit and with our inner selves.

🍁 *TOOL:*
(1) Creative Ways to Add Silence to Your Life
(p. 151)

PRACTICING A DAILY SPIRITUAL RITUAL

When we dance, the journey itself is the point,
as when we play music the playing itself is the point.
And exactly the same thing is true in meditation.
Meditation is the discovery that the point of life
is always arrived at in the immediate moment.
Alan Watts, Philosopher (1915-1973)

It was a difficult time in my life. Routinely working 12-hour-days, 7-days-a-week at a high stress job over a period of several years had taken its toll on my physical health and emotional stability. Suffering with high blood pressure, a frozen shoulder and periodic gall bladder attacks, it was becoming a common occurrence for me to lose patience with my boss and engage in angry outbursts. By the fall of 1992, having worked almost five years on this job, I knew I had to do something to create some balance in my life if I wanted to regain my physical and emotional health.

Having read a couple of articles on the healing power of meditation, I thought it might be beneficial to add this spiritual ritual to my daily routine. But how could I do that? I already felt as if there were not enough hours in the day. Yet, intuitively I had a glimmering of hope that meditation might somehow help to reverse

realize when I take the time to consciously connect with Spirit on a daily basis, I tap into a level of calmness, introspection and peace. This makes a difference in my energy field which produces a ripple effect in my environment. I feel my daily spiritual ritual is a gift I give myself and, by extension, a gift I give to those around me.

 TOOL:

(5) Meditation Techniques *(p. 163)*

CREATING A SACRED SPACE

*Your sacred space is where you can
find yourself again and again.*
Joseph Campbell (1904-1987)

A fter my spiritual awakening in 1991 I began to meet people who told me they had set aside a space in their home to be used strictly for meditation and finding solitude — a sacred space. Since I had a spare bedroom, I decided to use it to create a meditation room. I made an altar out of the top of an old hutch and covered it with a beautiful cloth. I bought some nice candles to place on top of the altar and made it a practice to go into this room each day to pray, write, read and meditate. This simple act changed my own energy as well as the energy of my house.

A few months later I agreed to rent my spare bedroom to someone who needed a place to stay. As a result, I had to give up my sacred space. This did not feel good to me, so I did something that actually horrified my daughter. I sold all my "family room" furniture, moved my "good" living room furniture into the family room and made my living room into my sacred space. Because my living room was open and visible to people walking in the front door, I bought oriental screens to block the view and keep the space private. I created a big altar with lots of candles and crystals and decorated the room with large floor pillows, beautiful plants and sacred pictures.

As my healing work expanded to include a form of emotional release bodywork, I began to use this bigger room to work with my clients. It truly became a treasured sacred space.

Early one morning during my daily meditation, I asked for guidance about a three-day intensive workshop I would be attending in a few days. Specifically, I wanted to know what this workshop would mean for me. With my eyes closed, I sat on a floor pillow about five feet away from the altar silently waiting for an answer.

When I opened my eyes, I noticed what appeared to be a leaf on the floor a few feet from the pillow on which I was sitting. Staring at the leaf I thought, "That leaf really looks like a frog." I continued to stay in my meditative state staring at the leaf. I then began to wonder how the leaf got there. All my plants were located too far away for a leaf to have dropped and landed anywhere near my altar. Again, I thought about the leaf looking like a frog and decided to reach out and pick it up. As I did, the "leaf" *jumped* toward me. Startled, I let out a little scream as I discovered the "leaf" was, indeed, a frog!!

My meditation was over. I spent the next few minutes trying to catch the frog as it jumped all around the meditation room. I finally caught it by dropping a scarf on top of it, closing the scarf and depositing my "messenger" safely outside. Remembering my question, *"what would this workshop mean to me,"* I called a friend who was familiar with animal totems. I asked her what was meant by the appearance of a frog. She replied with one word, "Transformation."

I had my answer. The workshop did prove to be a transformational event in my life and to this day, I have no idea how a frog could have found its way into my home. And, I guess it really isn't important for me to know. It came in some magical way to deliver an answer to my question.

When Victor and I got together, we decided to move the meditation room once again to a spare bedroom. Together we created a beautiful space and agreed we would use it only for meditation, for solitude when we felt the need, and for processing any issues that came up between us. The first year we were together we used it often to process our feelings, growing in our trust and love for one another. After more than 15 years together, our meditation room continues to be our sanctuary. Even though we both work at home and typically spend most of each day together, the time we spend every morning in our sacred space is the focal point of our day: centering us, nourishing our souls and helping us to achieve and maintain a state of inner peace.

TOOLS:
(4) Create Your Sacred Space *(p. 159)*
(5) Meditation Techniques *(p. 163)*

STORY 4

MOVING YOUR BODY

The body is a sacred garment.
Dance is the hidden language of the soul.
Martha Graham, Choreographer (1894-1991)

When I am emotionally or mentally stuck, I often find relief and release by consciously moving my body. I turn on some inspirational music, close my eyes and simply let the music move me. In this space, I often experience feeling as if I AM the music.

On one occasion, this process provided a profound healing experience. For several months our normally quiet neighborhood had been experiencing problems with teenagers having loud, unruly parties, often turning into street fights right under my bedroom window. Also at this same time there was a family in the neighborhood who had loud and sometimes violent domestic quarrels. It was a common occurrence for the police to be called to quell the disturbances. This situation was having a serious impact on my neighborhood as well as on my feeling of safety and security.

Early one morning around four o'clock I woke to the rhythmic beating of a gentle rain on the roof. Earlier in the evening there had been a neighborhood disturbance complete with squad cars and sirens. At this early morning hour with the rain gently falling I decided to get up to meditate and try to move all negative emotions I was feeling out of my body.

I turned on a favorite tape and with my eyes closed began to sway to the music — the sound of the rain keeping a steady background rhythm. Soon I felt my heart filling with love as my body moved and my mind began to meld into the music. Then something mystical happened. I began to envision my love encapsulated in each raindrop falling on my neighborhood. I actually felt "being the rain." I continued to "rain love" on my neighborhood for the duration of my meditation. It was a truly beautiful experience. I then returned to bed and went back to sleep.

When I awoke a few hours later I felt something had shifted. I knew energetically something was different and I was imbued with a feeling of lightness. A few days later the couple with the domestic problems moved away. I have no idea what happened to the partying teens, but following my "rain dance" there was never another teen disturbance in the neighborhood.

I had energetically moved some negativity out of my body while embracing the whole experience in love and, as I healed, the neighborhood healed.

❦ *TOOL:*
(5) Meditation Techniques *(p. 163)*

STORY 5

WORKING YOUR JOY

If everyone worked their joy, there would be
no unemployment on this planet.
Matthew Fox, Theologian (1940 -)

When I accepted a position in 1989 as office manager for a small engineering firm, I thought I had hit the jackpot! The office was just ten minutes from my home, which eliminated my daily two-hour commute to and from San Francisco. In addition, the salary offered was almost twice as much as I was currently earning. Because the job was so close to home, I looked forward to being able to spend more time with my kids. What was not disclosed at the time of the interview was an important fact: I would often be expected to work twelve-hour days sometimes seven days a week.

In addition to the long hours, the job itself was extremely stressful. As a result, my emotional and physical state began to deteriorate. During the first year I gained over fifty pounds. When my weight reached 230 I stopped weighing myself. My blood pressure rose to 160 over 102 eventually prompting my doctor to put me on medication to lower my blood pressure. My cholesterol rose to almost 300. I ruptured two disks in my neck resulting in a frozen shoulder and for almost a year I was

I started to open his office door, when I turned back to him and asked, "Tell me, what have you decided about my four-day workweek request?"

He gave me a blank look and then waived his hand in a dismissive manner saying, "Oh that… I haven't given it a thought."

As I heard those words something inside me snapped. I gently closed his office door and walked back to the front of his desk. He looked up at me as I said to him, "You know, I have thought of little else since I made my request. And, if you had said, *'Carol, there is no way I can give you a four-day workweek right now, we are so busy,'* I would have understood. We are busier in this office than we have ever been and I would have understood. On the other hand, if you had said, *'OK, let's give it a try,'* that probably wouldn't have worked. Knowing you the way I do, you would probably conjure up some emergency on my day off and call me in. If I wasn't available, you would make sure I felt guilty, and pretty soon I would be back to working the hours I'm working now. So, that wouldn't have worked. However, based on you ***'not giving it a thought'*** (and I waived my hand the way he had) you have my resignation!"

Let me be clear about this. I had not gone to work on Christmas Eve intending to resign my job. I had no money in the bank; I was $30,000 in debt; and, I had no other job prospects. So, when those unexpected words came out of my mouth, I literally jumped out of my body, thinking, ***"Who is talking for me?"***

My shocked boss looked at me in disbelief and exclaimed, "**WHAT?**"

I found myself saying in a low, deliberate, measured voice, "You are eating me alive and I will no longer sell my soul to this company."

Still in a state of disbelief, he asked, "What are you going to do?"

"I have no idea," I replied. "I don't have another job. All I know is that whatever I do, it's going to be something spiritual."

Well, again a shock wave pulsed through me. Now I **knew** someone was talking for me, because I had never said or even thought those words.

My boss was incredulous. He blurted out, "*SPIRITUAL!?!?*" (*Understand — this was a typical engineering firm, hardly a spiritual environment.*)

Continuing in a disbelieving tone, he asked, "And just when are you planning to do this?"

Not having intended to resign at all, I had not actually thought it through, so I said the first thing that came to mind, "On my birthday. You have six weeks."

After making my unexpected announcement, I walked out of his office and went home. My knees were shaking and my mind was racing with all the ramifications of what I had just done. On one level, I felt a degree of panic and yet on another level I was surprisingly calm and centered.

In those days I used to read the Tarot as a hobby and had been in the practice of pulling a card from the Medicine Woman deck each morning before going to work. That morning, for some reason, I had neglected to pull a card. So, the first thing I did when I got home was to spread out the deck and carefully pull a card. Looking it up in the book I was gratified to read its meaning: "You have long sought your freedom and today you have achieved it." I sighed and thought, *"Well, that feels like a really good sign."*

The day after Christmas I met a man who invited me to attend a twenty-four hour meditation on New Year's Eve. I accepted the invitation and in the week between Christmas and New Year's I began to meditate on what brings me joy. I had not yet crystallized that in my heart and I knew I didn't have much time. What came to me was, *healing work* brings me joy. But I knew I could never be a healer until I healed myself. I had always hated my body. Even as a little girl I can remember wishing I had a different body. I knew I had to somehow accept my body the way it was and learn to love it unconditionally before I could ever be a healer.

So, during the New Year's Eve meditation, I prayed the same prayer over and over again for twenty-four hours. *"God, give me a tool that will bring body, mind and spirit into alignment. Give me a tool that will enable me to love **me** just the way I am."* The tool I was given in that meditation is the process I now call "Lighten Up," an easy five-minute-a-day transformational tool responsible for changing my life in so many ways.

My last day at the engineering firm was set for February 12th. On January 23rd I was introduced to Diamond Trammel who asked me to co-partner a new alternative healing center in Pleasant Hill, California with her. We opened the center on March 1, 1993, starting out with two healing rooms, a small workshop space, a small bookstore and four practitioners. Within three months we had expanded to seven healing rooms and twelve practitioners. Within nine months we had expanded to nine healing rooms and thirty-two practitioners. I personally used the Center to do my healing work *(Reiki)* and eventually to teach Lighten Up classes several times a week.

I stayed at Reunion Center for three years during which time I grew in many ways. My work has continued to evolve and the Universe has continued to support me as I work my joy. I am deeply grateful to Matthew Fox for reaching into my heart and touching my soul. His message was exactly what I needed. It helped me summon the courage to take the risk I needed to take at that point along my life's path. Quitting the job at the engineering firm was the first empowering step I took in the journey of aligning with my Divine purpose.

Two years after I quit my job I had the opportunity to once again attend a Matt Fox lecture. At the end of the talk he invited the audience to ask questions. I raised my hand and told him I had attended his talk two years prior and, as a direct result of his talk, I had quit my job.

He put his hand over his heart and took a step backward almost as if someone had pushed him. I quickly assured him, "It was the **best** step I have ever taken and I want to thank you for helping me find the courage to work my joy."

A little while later a woman in the audience asked, "Matthew, what is your definition of sin?"

Matt paused for a moment and then replied, "Sin is seeing your next step and not taking it. This woman," he said, pointing to me, "saw her next step. If she had not taken it, that would have been a sin."

✳ *TOOLS:*

  (2) Find Your Joy Exercise *(p. 155)*
  (8) Lighten Up Process *(p. 175)*

LOVING YOURSELF

*If you seek love outside yourself
you can be certain that you perceive hatred within,
and are afraid of it. (A Course in Miracles)*

Scripture instructs us to "Love your neighbor as yourself." I believe this is one of our most important commandments. I also believe everyone on this planet obeys this commandment, to the letter, without any effort whatsoever!

You might be surprised by this statement as your mind leaps to all the wars and violence and suffering in the world — sure indicators people certainly don't love their neighbors as themselves.

However, by shifting our perception to a realization that most of us have never been taught, and thus have never learned, to love *ourselves* — we can now understand how we *are* obeying this commandment. We have been taught: it is selfish to love ourselves; we are bad if we love ourselves; we are not lovable unless we look a certain way or behave in a "normal" manner. Therefore, we have been conditioned since childhood to look at ourselves with negativity and even hate. I believe there is a direct correlation between the amount of violence in the world and the huge number of people who do not love themselves!

Many spiritual teachers and healers have written about the importance of self-love. However, few, if any, have given their readers a clear method or process to achieve this goal — a state of unconditional love of self. After you finish reading the information they present you are left with the question: "But how can I love myself when every time I look in the mirror I see an image I don't respect, appreciate, admire, cherish or love?"

Until 1993, I was one of those people who did not love myself, particularly my body. As a little girl I can remember wishing I had a different body and as an adult I was so ashamed of my naked body, I could not look at it in a mirror. I was extremely overweight and in poor health with high blood pressure and high cholesterol.

Then a miracle happened. During a twenty-four hour meditation beginning on New Year's Eve, 1992, I prayed the same prayer over and over again: "God, give me a tool that will bring body, mind and spirit into alignment. Give me a tool that will enable **me** to love **me**, just the way I am."

In the silence of meditation my prayer was answered. A small, still voice instructed me to do a simple daily process I came to call "Lighten Up." The process was so simple and easy, my mind immediately wanted to discount it. However, the quiet voice had been so specific and clear, something inside of me **knew** this was an important step for me to take.

I started doing the process every day without any expectations whatsoever — I just did it every day.

About a month into the process I noticed my clothes were getting loose on me and I thought, "I wonder if I'm losing weight?" I got on the scale and found I had lost 17 pounds. This was really surprising to me, as I was not consciously doing anything to make myself lose weight.

About two weeks into the process I ran out of blood pressure medication. I decided not to refill my prescription because I knew I had a physical coming up in two weeks and I wanted to see if the meditation I had begun doing every morning was having any effect.

At my checkup, the doctor took my blood pressure and got a quizzical look on her face. She said, "I'm not getting a very good reading in that arm. I'd better take it on the other arm." She took my blood pressure on my left arm and asked, "What have you been doing?"

"What do you mean?" I replied.

Without answering my question, she asked, "Have you been exercising?"

"Nope, not me," I said.

"Well, you've been doing **something**. Your blood pressure is 116 over 67," she stated. "What have you been doing?"

I admitted to her, "I haven't been taking my medication for the past couple of weeks, and I have also started meditating."

Her response surprised me. "I believe so much in meditation to help control blood pressure," she said, "but most patients don't believe me and want a pill instead. I see no reason for you to go back on medication. Just continue doing what you're doing and we'll keep an eye on your blood pressure to make sure it's stabilized."

A week later we got my cholesterol test results. It had dropped from 300 to 167. All this was happening without any conscious change of diet, and I still wasn't associating any of these changes with the simple "loving" process I was doing every day.

I was, however, curious about why I was experiencing these changes. So I started asking in meditation why these changes were happening. What came to me was to look at **what** I was eating and **how** I was eating. I decided to start an "eating diary" noting everything I ate throughout the day.

In studying my diary after about a week, I was surprised to find my diet had changed dramatically since the first of the year. I realized, without conscious effort, I had eliminated sugar from my diet. I had been what I would call a "sugar-holic" all my life. I would buy a box of cookies thinking I would eat one or two, but would invariably end up eating the whole box once I started. I would buy a half-gallon of ice cream and would finish it off in a couple of days. Also, every afternoon at three o'clock I had to have a candy bar break. I was shocked when I realized, since the first of January I had not eaten even one candy bar! I had **not** consciously decided to stop eating candy bars — I simply no longer thought about it. I also realized, I was no longer buying cookies and that there was a half-gallon of my favorite ice cream in the freezer I had not even been tempted to open.

However, a dramatic realization that something out of the ordinary was happening with my diet and sugar occurred one day when a co-worker had a birthday. I decided to buy **my** favorite cheesecake for an office celebration. The staff arrived at the appointed time in the conference room and after singing "happy birthday," my friend proceeded to cut me a great big piece of cake. I found myself saying, "Oh, I can't eat such a big piece. Cut it in half." She cut it in half and when she handed it to me my body recoiled. I found I could not put even **one** bite of the cake into my mouth. I knew something was up! This was my *favorite* cheesecake and in the past I could have easily eaten two or three pieces. Now, all of a sudden, the thought of eating something so rich and sweet upset my stomach. I really didn't understand what was going on.

Also while analyzing my diet, I realized I had not eaten any meat since the first of the year. I had given up red meat in 1976 but I still ate chicken and turkey. All of a sudden it dawned on me — I had become a vegetarian without making a conscious decision to do so. This was a startling revelation.

The only thing I had consciously given up as a New Year's resolution was caffeine. I typically drank three to five cups of coffee a day and two or three cokes a day. I had tried giving up coffee on many occasions and had never been successful. So, when I made this New Year's resolution, I knew what to expect: a week or two of caffeine withdrawal headaches and an overwhelming desire to drink my favorite beverages. Although I did get the headaches, the difference this time was I never experienced a desire for a cup of coffee or a coke. This was amazing!! I was working in an environment where coffee was being brewed all day. The smell of coffee was in the air. People around me were drinking coffee and setting their cups on my desk. The coke machine was a few steps from my office. But I never again **desired** another cup of coffee or a coke.

When I told this story in one of my workshops, a participant exclaimed, "Well, I'm **not** giving up my coffee!" I said to him, "I'm not asking you to give up anything."

Still not satisfied, he grumbled, "I get up every morning and grind my beans and if I couldn't start my day with my cup of coffee, I couldn't start my day!"

I reiterated, "This is not a process of deprivation and I'm not asking you to give up anything."

As I could hear him still grumbling, I couldn't help smiling while I told him he needed to "lighten up!"

Two weeks later on a Saturday I got a call from this guy. He said almost sheepishly, "I just want you to know, I haven't had any coffee since Wednesday."

Surprised, I queried, "You haven't? And you don't have any headaches?"

"**Yes, I have headaches**," he said, almost shouting into the phone. "I have a headache right now. But I don't want any coffee and I just don't understand it. I woke up on Wednesday morning and I just didn't want any coffee."

Then in a quieter voice he hesitantly asked, "Do you think it's that damn lotion I've been spreading on my body?"

I could barely contain my amusement. He was trying to blame his change in behavior on the lotion he was using as part of his Lighten Up process, instead of realizing it was the process itself causing the change. I simply chuckled and said, "Well, it could be…"

I like to share this story to emphasize that Lighten Up is **not** a process of deprivation. It is a process of love, bringing body, mind and spirit into alignment. I believe when we go into an emotional state of deprivation, we are not in alignment. Alignment between body, mind and spirit requires cooperation, and deprivation does not form the basis for cooperation.

 TOOL:
   (8) Lighten Up Process *(p. 175)*

The voice responded, "**No**, that's **not** what it's all about. Once they experience unconditional love of self, they can for the first time love others unconditionally. They can't do that until they love themselves unconditionally."

I took a really deep breath and thought, "Yup, that's the big picture."

More gently, the voice continued, "No, that's **not** the big picture. Once they love others unconditionally, you will experience **true** world peace. **That's** the picture!"

This experience literally took my breath away. I needed to sit for a while to digest what had just been revealed to me. I had always viewed Lighten Up through the small window of self-love. I had never carried forward the ripple effect of what it means to love yourself. I now understood the big picture. If everyone loved themselves unconditionally, everyone would love others unconditionally and we **would** experience world peace!

Because we are all connected, as each of us begins the healing process on ourselves, we automatically help to heal others. By helping to heal others, we help to heal the planet. So if you ever get discouraged doing the Lighten Up process, or your mind insists you don't have time, or tries to make you believe you are just not worth the effort, remember the Big Picture. Do the process for world peace. As you heal yourself, you are creating a ripple effect helping everyone on the planet to heal — a very unselfish motive indeed!

After I gave the preceding example at one of my workshops, a class participant said how helpful it was to
her. Being able to frame her daily Lighten Up ritual of
moisturizing herself as contributing to the larger goal of
world peace was just the motivation she needed to do
the process. Another participant then chimed in and
suggested I might want to consider promoting Lighten
Up by making some "Moisturize for Peace" bumper
stickers. We all had a big laugh!

✹ *TOOLS:*

(5) Meditation Techniques *(p. 163)*
(8) Lighten Up Process *(p. 175)*

PAYING ATTENTION TO THE SIGNALS

Unfurl yourself into the grace of beginning
That is at one with your life's desire.
Awaken your spirit to adventure;
Hold nothing back, learn to find ease in risk;
Soon you will be home in a new rhythm,
For your soul senses the world that awaits you.
- Excerpt from "For A New Beginning," by John O'Donohue

*W*hen the time for change comes into our lives, it is not always easy to see the wisdom of embracing the change. I had always been someone who would set goals for myself and if something came along looking as if it would cause me to change direction, I would often dig in my heels and try even harder to achieve the goal in the way I had pre-determined was the "right path." I rarely would change direction until it became almost impossible to keep going in the direction I had chosen. This, of course, would invariably create a great deal of havoc in my life. I have now learned to pay attention and listen to those quiet and often subtle voices of change and the wisdom of taking action **before** the voices become **loud** messages. I have learned to recognize when I am no longer "in the flow."

In the three and a half years I worked as one of the coordinators at the Reunion Center, I learned many lessons about change. One lesson I learned was life is not meant to be a struggle and if we stay in the flow it never is a struggle. When it does become a struggle, this is usually a sign we need to surrender control and trust in the perfection of all things. We then bring ourselves back into the flow.

In 1993 I was given the opportunity to partner with Diamond Trammel and open an alternative healing center we called the Reunion Center of Light. We brought with us a shared vision for the Center and complimentary skills to implement our vision. Diamond had amazing decorating skills and I had computer and graphic design skills. Diamond created an exquisitely beautiful center filled with a wonderful nurturing energy. I created the many business forms we needed, managed our database, ran our small bookstore and produced our newsletter, *The Beacon*, which "got us out there." Within a year we grew from three rooms to nine rooms and from four practitioners to over thirty practitioners. As we expanded, Diamond and I always felt we were "in the flow." The few "rapids" we did encounter in the stream were short lived and added a new dimension to our journey.

In 1996, however, I started to notice my life had become somewhat of a struggle around my responsibilities at the Center. I had met Victor and we were spending a great deal of time traveling around the country presenting our Lighten Up workshop. Diamond and I realized we were on different timetables in our lives. As I found my life rapidly expanding and changing, my vision for the Center became different from Diamond's vision. We were no longer in alignment.

Putting our spiritual principles to work, Diamond and I came to a decision — it was time for me to step away from my role at the Center. This was done with love and understanding for each other's path. If we had decided to operate in the old paradigm of "control" and "attachment" we could have made a big issue out of "who was right" and stayed in there for the "fight." However, we both realized in our hearts, it was for the highest good of the Center, as well as in my highest good, for me to let go of my position as Center coordinator.

Throughout this transition period I continued to be reminded of the words of my dear friend Greg Tamblyn in one of his witty songs, "If the signals are flashing and the gates are all down, and the whistle is blowing in vain, if you stay on the tracks, ignoring the facts, then you can't blame the wreck on the train." Diamond and I both wanted to avoid "a wreck," so we took the necessary steps to keep the Center on track and intact.

The Reunion Center had been for me like a nurturing cocoon where I had been held in a safety zone to grow and expand. Without the Center, my growth would not have been as easy or probably as fast. Without the Center I would not have had the vehicle to grow "Lighten Up" and I probably would never have met Victor. To say I am grateful for the gifts the Center gave me seems inadequate.

However, when my struggling began, I realized it was time for me to emerge from my cocoon and fly with the wings of a butterfly. I knew in my heart, as I let go of my responsibilities the right and perfect people would show up to help Diamond continue the work of the Center. And they did.

❧ TOOL:

(18) 5-Chapter Story *(p. 205)*

LETTING GO OF JUDGMENTS

*The major block to compassion is
the judgment in our minds.
Judgment is the mind's primary tool of separation.
~Rev. Diane Berke, Ph.D.*

*M*any years ago I was involved in a process geared to help me get in touch with my judgments and to become aware of how many passed through my mind on a daily basis. Judgments are those thoughts that seem to automatically surface when someone doesn't fit my idea of "normal" or when I hear an idea outside of "my box."

In following the requirements of the process, I carried a small notebook around with me for a week making a tick mark in it each time I had a judgmental thought. By the end of the first day I was amazed to discover I had over 150 tick marks in my notebook! As I continued to monitor my judgments, my tick marks decreased each day and by the last day of the week I had only four!

Judgments Keep Us in a State of Separation

Participating in this exercise made me realize that most of the judgmental thoughts I had were not my own, but thoughts and beliefs I had acquired from my parents or my peers who probably acquired them in like manner. I also realized the judgments I held in most cases were **not** the truth. They were merely thoughts I had anchored in my consciousness over the years keeping me *separate* from others.

After all, most judgments are, in reality, personal attacks fostering separation (i.e., *"he's so lazy he'll never amount to anything"* or *"she is so irresponsible"* or *"they are a bunch of idiots"* and so on). This, in turn, inhibits us from going below the surface of our judgments to reach a place of understanding. If we take the time to examine the judgment, we might be able to actually get in touch with the real thought. For instance, the thought beneath, "She is so irresponsible" might actually be, "I'm afraid for her — she may end up hurting herself or others." Or it could mean, "She makes me angry because I can't count on her to keep her word."

When we stay in judgment, it is difficult, if not impossible, to resolve the many issues confronting or challenging us. However, when we take the time to uncover the true thought under the judgment, we can then shift from reactive mode to compassionate mode, enabling us to take the appropriate action from a place of honesty and integrity. This idea is further explored in the Tools: Letting Go of Judgments Exercise and Free Yourself from Fear Process.

We not only have judgmental thoughts about others, many of us also judge ourselves negatively. Perhaps we may find ourselves thinking, *"I sure am stupid"* or *"I don't ever get anything right"* or *"I'm not as good as they are"* or *"I'll never be successful"* and so on. As I teach in the Free Yourself from Fear process: thought is **the** creative energy. When we allow these judgmental and limiting thoughts to rattle around in our consciousness, they create our reality. When we change our thought patterns, we change our lives.

✸ *Judgments Keep Us in a State of Negativity*

I think of judgments and criticism in the same light. All of us have probably found ourselves in situations where the favorite pastime is to sit around and complain. This often happens in a work environment. Being in such an environment saps our energy. We go home feeling drained and in many cases angry — and we don't even understand why.

We can each make a difference in such a situation by consciously refusing to participate in judgments and criticism — by assessing the situation, not the person. When we intentionally begin to eliminate judgments from our consciousness, we change our energy and raise our vibration. And when our energy changes, it affects the energy of those around us.

When I was going through my judgment exercise, my boss made a disparaging remark to me about the inefficiency of the support staff in producing a report that had to be finished by the end of the day. He often made these types of remarks when we were facing deadlines and I normally responded in an angry and defensive manner, which of course, never helped the situation.

This time, however, instead of taking his remark personally, I responded by calmly giving him an honest assessment of the situation, the obstacles the support staff was facing and how we could work through them to get the report done on time if we all cooperated. He was so taken aback by my calmness and change of attitude, he looked at me quizzically and said, "And what workshop did you attend last weekend?"

Because of the shift in my attitude, from then on my relationship with my boss became more positive and created a shift in his attitude not only toward me but also toward the entire support staff. This changed the way the support staff felt about their jobs. They became happier and more productive. This had the ripple effect of changing the energy between the support staff and the engineers which in turn changed the energy of the entire office.

I have found letting go of judgments to be a valuable personal growth tool as well as a way to create a positive ripple effect of love and understanding. There is no down side to letting go of judgments.

❧ TOOLS:

(9) Free Yourself from Fear Process *(p. 181)*
(10) Rainbow Clearing Exercise *(p. 185)*
(11) Letting Go of Judgments Exercise *(p. 187)*

ROWING YOUR OWN BOAT

There is an underlying current in your life –
a divine flow – that is continually guiding you toward
the effortless fulfillment of your heart's desires.
Steven Lane Taylor, Author

This story comes from listening to one of Wayne Dyer's many tapes. He tells the story of singing *Row, Row, Row Your Boat* with his young child in their swimming pool. As the two were singing, he realized this children's song was actually a metaphysical lesson.

"Listen," he says. "Row, row, row, **your** boat. Not your spouse's boat, not your kid's boat, not your friend's boat. **Your** boat."

"**Gently**," he says. "We're not being instructed to **struggle**, we are being told to be gentle."

"**Down** the stream," he continues. "Notice, it doesn't say to row **up** stream — that would be a struggle. We are being instructed to stay in the flow and row **down** the stream."

"**Merrily, merrily, merrily**," he laughs. "We are being instructed to have fun, don't take life so seriously, because..."

"Life is but a dream," he concludes. "Isn't it?"

This little bit of wisdom changed the way I do my life. I used to be one of those people who would set a goal and come hell or high water I would work toward achieving the goal even if all indications pointed to the fact I was rowing upstream. In fact, the harder it got, the more I would hang on, determined to carry on the struggle.

After listening to Wayne Dyer's story, I realized there was another way. Now, every time I notice I am beginning to struggle with something in my life, I realize I am not in the flow. I look at what I'm doing and make the necessary adjustments to get back into the flow. This may involve using the Free Yourself process to transform some thoughts. It also may involve using the 5-Chapter Story to determine where I am in my process. Or, it may simply involve clearing myself.

When you notice you are struggling, it doesn't necessarily mean you need to give up your goal. It may mean you simply need to take a different path to achieve the goal. What is important is to pay attention to your process. If you are not having fun and life has become a struggle, it's time to change course and get back in the flow.

✺ *TOOLS:*
(9) Free Yourself from Fear Process *(p. 181)*
(10) Rainbow Clearing Exercise *(p. 185)*
(18) The 5-Chapter Story Exercise *(p. 205)*

TELLING THE TRUTH

The truth which has made us free
will in the end make us glad also.
~Felix Adler (1851-1933)

One of the most important lessons I am learning in this lifetime is the importance of expressing my truth and allowing others to express theirs without judgment. Years ago I attended a workshop called Loving Communications. It taught the concept, "all truths are true." By this they meant, when a person is expressing something from their heart, whether or not it resonates as your truth is not the issue. Their expression is their truth. It is valid for them and deserves to be heard. With this understanding I can be tolerant, non-emotional and non-judgmental when discussing belief systems with others. I can fully hear them and at the same time be the observer and detach from emotional involvement in their truth.

Expressing my own truth has been a more difficult lesson for me, however. When Victor and I entered into our wonderful relationship we took only one vow. It wasn't a vow of undying love or a vow we would be there for each other for eternity. It was a vow to always express our truth, even at the expense of possibly hurting the other person's feelings.

STORY 12

CONNECTING WITH YOUR
SUBCONSCIOUS HEALER

"Whatever we plant in our subconscious mind
and nourish with repetition and emotion
will one day become a reality."
Earl Nightingale (1921-1989)

Almost everyone has a story to tell about how an unexpected event in their lives answered a question or helped bring some degree of clarity or enlightenment. This is one of those stories.

I love to read and one of my favorite past-times is browsing in bookstores. During one such excursion, a book literally fell off a shelf right at my feet. I picked it up and read the title, "Instant ESP" by David St. Clair.

Laughing to myself, I thought, "Who would buy a book like this?"

Before putting it back on the shelf, however, I fanned the pages ever so quickly. Something in the book caught my attention — a chapter about your subconscious healer. I read a few paragraphs and turned to the back cover to check out the price of the book. Seeing it was only $3.95, I thought, "Well, for $3.95, I'll buy this book."

The book was filled with many interesting techniques, but the one I found most intriguing described a way to communicate with your subconscious to heal bodily ailments. The technique involves visualizing your subconscious as a person residing in your body whose only job is to take care of your body and do your bidding. Your subconscious takes care of all the things in your body you never think about (i.e., breathing, heartbeat, organ functions, etc.) and is also available to take care of any ailments going on in your body. You need only to give your subconscious the order to do so.

The following story illustrates my first experience in using this powerful process:

I had a bunion on my right foot which had bothered me for over a year. The bunion hurt only when I was driving my car and then it felt like a hot poker drilling through my foot. My doctor had indicated surgery was my only option.

So after reading about this technique, I decided, while driving to work on a Monday morning, to give my subconscious the order to cure the bunion. As the book instructed, I gave the order to my subconscious by saying three times out loud, "You know what is causing this pain in my right foot, make it go away!" The pain did not go away.

Driving home from work that day my foot again started hurting and again I gave the order three times out loud. The pain did not go away. On Tuesday morning, again I tried. The pain did not go away.

On Friday morning I was driving to work and noticed my foot was not hurting. I had to think back to remember when I had last experienced the pain. It was Tuesday morning, the third time I had given the order.

"Well," I thought, "I can always make it hurt."

When I arrived at my office, I pulled off my shoe and felt where the bunion had been. There was no bump, and no matter how hard I pushed, I could not make my foot hurt. Just then a co-worker came into my office and told me she was experiencing a sharp pain in the back of her left shoulder. I told her about the technique. Giving me a funny look, she said nothing in reply as she turned and left my office.

About 15 minutes later she came back very excited. She said she had gone into the restroom, had tried the technique and the pain had gone away.

"All I feel now," she said, "is a sensation of warmth where the pain used to be."

I caught my breath. I had forgotten it had said in the book, "You may feel warmth in the area when the healing takes place."

I have shared this technique with many people over the years and the results have been phenomenal. I encourage you to give it a try. It certainly is a safe and very affordable healing tool with no negative side effects.

As a side note to the story: My co-worker decided she wanted to purchase the book, so she went to the bookstore where I had bought my copy. She could not find it on the shelf, so she asked the cashier to look it up for her. He looked it up in the database and told her the book had been out of print for years.

"Well, my friend just bought a copy of it in this bookstore last week," she told the clerk.

The clerk shook his head and said, "You must be mistaken. Your friend could **not** have purchased it here. We don't deal in used books and as I said the book has been out of print for years."

✹ *TOOL:*

(3) Subconscious Healer Exercise *(p. 157)*

ATTRACTING YOUR HEART'S DESIRE USING THE LAW OF ATTRACTION

Your Inner Being would want you to manifest everything that you decide that you want. Your Inner Being would want you to know that you have value and the ability to have or be or do anything. Your Inner Being would want you to fulfill every wish and whim that you could identify.
~ Abraham

In 1985 my twenty-year marriage ended in an amicable divorce and I moved from Wisconsin to California with my three children. After about ten years of being a single mom, I decided it was time for me to have a man in my life. Since I was on a conscious spiritual path, I decided I to use my metaphysical principles to manifest the "perfect" man.

The process I chose to use was described in an Abraham-Hicks tape I had been given. Everyday for twenty minutes I would go into my "manifesting workshop." With pad and pen handy, I made a list of everything I wanted in a relationship: an intelligent man who is on a conscious spiritual path; a truthful man who is willing to grow along with me; a man who will work along side me and be the "wind under my wings;" a man who is fun and comfortable to be around, a man who listens—really listens; a man who is wise and understanding; a man who is compassionate, caring and nurturing.

I desired a relationship with a man who loves to travel and meet exciting and interesting people. I desired a relationship in which we shared mutual appreciation and respect for one another.

During the day I gathered "data" by observing other couples and making mental notes about how they interacted and what appealed to me. Then every morning I added to and refined my list.

About three weeks into the exercise, wonderful men started showing up in my life. They met almost all of my "requirements;" however, they were all gay. I had to refine my list. I added, "I want a heterosexual man." Young men in their twenties and thirties started showing up in my life. Since I was then fifty, more refinements were definitely needed!

The last entry I made on my list was, "I want a man my age."

Three days later I was at a regularly attended monthly networking breakfast where everyone had an opportunity to introduce themselves to the group and tell something about their work. A man who was new to the group introduced himself as Victor Grey. He was a hypnotherapist who had recently moved to California from Connecticut and was looking for a place to do his work. After the introductions were over I sought him out, told him about the healing center I directed and invited him to take a tour. We made an appointment for the next day. He loved the center and joined the staff.

It was my practice to always invite a new staff member to attend my Lighten Up workshop as my guest. The next one was in a couple of days and Victor attended. After the workshop he thanked me and asked if he could repay my kindness by painting my portrait. *(Among his many talents, he is also an accomplished artist)*. I was thrilled to accept. We made an appointment for the next day.

After he finished my portrait we spent a couple hours talking and sharing life experiences. During the course of the conversation he just happened to mention he was fifty. I said, "Oh, you're my age."

As soon as those words came out of my mouth, my immediately thought was, "I wonder if this is the guy?"

The next day I left for Wisconsin for three weeks. While I was gone I kept wondering if Victor was "the guy." When I returned to California I called him to see how he was doing at the Center. He said he loved it and then he suggested we get together sometime. I told him I had invited an out-of-town guest over for dinner the next evening and asked if he would like to join us. He accepted the invitation. The three of us had a great evening and when my guest retired for the evening, Victor and I sat in my meditation room and talked until three o'clock in the morning. Three weeks later, he moved in with me.

Victor fulfilled every "requirement" on my list and more. He is spiritual, intelligent, caring, nurturing, kind and compassionate. He appreciates, honors and respects

Susan was guided to get in touch with the moment her illness began and to try to identify any event that may have occurred just prior to the onset of the illness. She remembered her illness had begun shortly after Andrea had confided in her. The healer guided Susan to get in touch with any emotions she had been experiencing since her illness. She realized she had been feeling extreme anger (particularly toward Andrea) as well as despair, helplessness, confusion and grief.

The healer then guided Susan to say the following: "Andrea, I got your experience. I got your anger, your despair, your helplessness, your confusion and your grief. I even got the physical manifestation of all these emotions. I now release myself from these emotions and I lovingly release you to your Divine Path."

Literally, within minutes Susan's symptoms disappeared and she again felt like herself. She had deprogrammed her system from Andrea's program (unexpressed emotions) and had reinstalled her own operating system. The anger she had been feeling in their relationship (which was really Andrea's suppressed anger expressing through Susan) was no longer running her.

One morning during our daily meditation, I had another opportunity to experience what it means to be someone's mirror. I found myself feeling some unexplained agitation toward Victor. I really couldn't put my finger on *why* I was feeling that way — I just noticed it. As we continued our meditation my agitation grew. I finally said to Victor, "I'm feeling angry at you and I don't know why." He closed his eyes, took a deep breath and said,

"You are probably feeling my anger at myself." He went on to explain he was upset with himself over a programming mistake he had made in a project he was working on. It then became clear to me I had been mirroring his anger. Using the Free Yourself process I helped him transform the thoughts fueling his anger and as he felt better, so did I.

I have found it is really important to learn to recognize whether our emotions are about something going on within ourselves or whether they may actually be an energy we are mirroring back to someone else.

So the question arises, how can we use this knowledge to cue into what within us needs healing? If everyone we meet is a mirror to us, then it becomes very important to pay attention to how we feel when we are around others. If I am with someone who makes me feel uncomfortable, it serves me to examine *why* I feel uncomfortable. I have a dear friend who enters into everything she does with child-like enthusiasm. She likes to sing and dance and act silly. Other friends seem to enjoy her exuberance, but being around her when she's acting in that way makes me feel extremely uncomfortable. I can always hear my judgmental self asking, "Why doesn't she act like an adult?"

I truly love this friend so it was important for me to examine why her behavior had such a negative effect on me. I decided to take it into meditation. What came to me was quite a surprise. I realized as I was growing up, I never really learned to be a "child." I cannot ever remember dancing around and giggling. It's not to say

I did not enjoy myself as a child, but I was always the "little lady" who acted "properly." I cannot say my parents expected that of me — I do not remember them ever criticizing me about my behavior. I think I just decided early on, I needed to act a certain way in order to be accepted. Now my friend was giving me a gift — a mirror to show me how I had effectively shut myself down as a child and it was now time to let my inner child out to play.

Being blessed with this insight, I find her behavior no longer troubles me and I am now able to find the place in me where my child-like joy resides. By taking the time to explore the gift of the mirror I was able to develop a deeper appreciation for my friend and also experience a personal healing.

❧ TOOLS:

(9) Free Yourself from Fear Process *(p. 181)*
(10) Rainbow Clearing Exercise *(p. 185)*
(12) Emotional Release Exercise *(p. 189)*
(13) Mirror Exercise *(p. 191)*

CLEARING YOURSELF

Taking on other people's energy
happens more easily than you might think!
~ Victor Grey, Lighten Up Workshop Co-facilitator

It can happen to any of us. We are feeling energized and in a great mood when for seemingly no reason we start feeling weary and out-of-sorts. Perhaps we have just attended a large, high-energy event and we have come away feeling drained. Or, we have spent an hour in a shopping mall and barely have the energy to drive home. One explanation for this shift in our energy could be that we may have taken on energy from others — energy that is not ours! Particularly vulnerable are people who are naturally empathic, people who work in healing fields (doctors, nurses, therapists), and people who touch others as part of their work (hair stylists, massage therapists, body workers, energy workers).

Energy, of course, is everywhere — we are swimming in a soup of unseen energy waves — and all of us pick up energy from people around us. So it is particularly useful to be aware of and to notice the signs when we may have picked up energy we need to release.

For several years I worked one-on-one with clients, helping them release negative emotions. I often came away from these sessions drained. Noticing this, Victor taught me a process he called the "rainbow clearing" that enabled me to release energy I had taken on. The process also works to clear away any negative energy we may have picked up interacting with others in the normal course of the day.

Often we do not recognize we have taken on an energy that has shifted us into a negative space. So it is very useful to have an agreement with someone you trust to remind you to clear yourself. Victor and I do this with each other whenever we notice one of us appears to be "out of sorts" or whenever we have been in a large group of people or in a public place and are feeling drained. Following are two stories illustrating how useful this tool can be.

The first story happened one evening when Victor and I stopped at a gas station. Victor got out of the car to fill the tank when all of a sudden I heard a man and woman yelling at each other. I turned around to see what the commotion was about but really could not make out what was going on. A few minutes later when Victor got back into the car, I asked him if he knew what had happened. He said the woman was yelling at the man because he had cut in front of her at the pump.

Victor started the car and pulled out into the street behind a car that was stopped at a stop sign. We waited a few seconds behind the car when Victor started yelling angrily at the driver in front of us to "get going." This was so out of character for Victor I turned to him and asked, "Have you cleared yourself?" He looked at me knowingly, closed his eyes, cleared himself and within seconds was back to his normal, calm and loving self. He had picked up the angry energy of the two people at the gas station and without realizing it had started exhibiting the same angry energy — energy that was not his! Being reminded to clear himself was the key to helping him release the unwanted energy.

The second story took place during a Lighten Up workshop Victor and I were presenting at a church. Most of the people in the audience were in the front rows. Just before we started our presentation a man entered and sat by himself near the back. About five minutes into our presentation this man interrupted us by shouting loudly, "Oh, God! Don't tell me this is about **weight loss**!"

Stopping in mid-sentence, I looked at him and replied, "No, it is **not** about weight loss, so please just hang in there with me."

He crossed his arms and his legs and glared at us throughout the first half of the workshop. His energy was doom and gloom and I found myself avoiding eye contact with him.

During the break this man came up to the front of the church and said angrily to Victor, "This workshop is **not** what I expected."

Victor replied, "I'm really sorry you are disappointed. I'm sure we can arrange to have your money refunded.

The man got louder and angrier. "It is **not** about money," he shouted. "You did not advertise this workshop correctly. It's not what I expected!"

Victor calmly answered, "I am truly sorry it's not what you expected, but it's what we are presenting and that can't be changed. Again, I will be happy to make arrangements to have your money refunded."

The man mumbled angrily as he stormed out, "I said it is **not** about the money!"

Well, Victor and I both cleared ourselves and assumed he would not be back after the break. Imagine our surprise when he walked in and once again took his seat in the back of the church assuming his cross-armed position. We continued with the second half of the workshop and came to the part where Victor leads the audience through the Rainbow Clearing exercise. The man actually followed the directions and participated in the exercise. As Victor guided the audience through the visualization, we were astonished when we saw the man physically convulse. His entire body shook. Both Victor and I looked at each other in amazement.

When we completed the exercise, the man looked like a different person. His body had relaxed and he no longer appeared angry.

At our workshops we always invite people to put their names in a basket for a drawing we hold at the end for a free copy of our Lighten Up tape. As our workshop ended, I asked a member of the audience to draw a name. She handed me the slip of paper and as I read the name, I looked up to see who would respond.

From the back of the room our angry participant, shyly waved his hand. I looked at him and somewhat painfully asked, "Do you want the prize?" After all — it was not the workshop he had expected. I was sure he would not want to bring home a recording of it.

He said in a quiet, calm voice, "I think the Universe is trying to give me a message."

After our workshops I always make myself available to talk one-on-one with members of the audience. Our door-prize winner waited patiently in line until everyone else had their turn. He then said to me, "I owe you an apology for my actions. All I can tell you is that I am a stockbroker and today the market crashed. I have been fielding calls all day from angry clients. I brought that energy in here with me and didn't even realize it until we did the Rainbow Clearing. I hope you can forgive me."

The next evening we were presenting the Free Yourself from Fear Workshop at the same church. Our door-prize winner from the previous evening was one of the first to arrive. I acknowledged him saying, "I didn't expect to see you here."

With a smile he said, "I would not have missed it for the world."

TOOL: (10) Rainbow Clearing Exercise *(p. 185)*

of the most important books on the planet." What a profound statement! I turned to Victor and said, "We need to study *A Course in Miracles*! Let's begin tomorrow morning." He agreed and thus began the most transformational journey of our lives.

We decided we could (and would) devote ten minutes the first thing each morning to *The Course*. I did not know what to expect but I was certainly full of great anticipation — I had heard from so many people about how wonderful *The Course* was.

So you can imagine my disappointment when I found I was really **hating** *The Course*. I was full of judgments about it! It was not easy to read or to understand and it was **so** male oriented — no mention whatsoever of the feminine! Why in the world would I want to spend my valuable time studying something that didn't honor the feminine?

After the first week or so, I expressed my disappointment and frustration to Victor, who seemed to actually be enjoying the process. He said to me gently, "You don't have to understand it. You don't even have to like it. All we have to do is to stick with it and I promise, it will change our lives." To be honest, I would have never continued had it not been for Victor's gentle steadfastness and loving encouragement to "stick with it."

The early edition of *The Course* we were using had been published as three books: *The Workbook*, *The Text*, and *The Manual for Teachers*. Victor felt it would be best for us to begin our journey by reading the smallest of the three books, *The Manual for Teachers*. It is in a question and answer format anticipating problems a student might have in understanding some of the principles presented (and I certainly did have some problems). We completed this book in a few days. Then we moved on to *The Workbook*, designed to take one year to complete. Each day we took turns reading the lesson for the day out loud to one another. Most of the lessons are short — from a couple of paragraphs to a couple of pages long. The lessons are, of course, just as the name implies — **lessons**. They are not meant to be simply read — they are meant to be practiced. This is where I met my resistance head-on. But with Victor's encouragement we stayed with *The Workbook* and completed it in a year, lesson by lesson.

About three months after we had started studying *The Workbook* I noticed a shift in my consciousness. I felt my judgments evaporating and found I was developing a great love for these teachings. I looked forward each morning to our meditation time. In fact, we both agreed it had become the most important time in our day. Although we started out by pledging to spend ten minutes each day in meditation, we now found we often spent thirty minutes or more.

I also noticed other areas of my life were changing. In addition to personally feeling a greater love of life, I realized our relationship with each other was deepening. Our meditation time was a catalyst that sparked creative ideas for every aspect of our lives, taking our relationship to a whole new level — from conscious to co-creative. As I look back to those early years I can now see how every creative idea Victor and I visualized and ultimately implemented came out of our meditation time together.

I can say, without reservation, studying *A Course in Miracles* is the most transformative process we, as a couple, have ever done for our relationship, as well as being the most transformative process I have ever done for myself personally.

❧ TOOLS:

BUILDING A BRIDGE
TO FIND THE COMMON GROUND

"Our Similarities bring us to a common ground;
Our Differences allow us to be fascinated by each other."
~ Tom Robbins, Author

I received the following email from a person who had registered to participate in the World Peace Experiment. After registering he had followed a link to my personal website where I have a great deal of information about my political views. Here is what he wrote:

> The "onlyloveprevails" site was so good and I liked your prayers, etc. that I submitted my name along with my wife's to make the 80,000. Then I went to your site and found something completely different (I guess I shouldn't have gone to the Politics page first). I am a supporter of President Bush AND of peace, but all I saw on that page was leftist propaganda garbage that did not seem to come from someone who meditates from A Course in Miracles. I hope someday you rise above duality consciousness and really represent a peace movement. I am not there yet either which is why the Politics page struck a bad chord.
>
> Peace, Lee

When I initially read his email, my first reaction was judgment and anger toward this man. I really do not like feeling that way, so I went into our meditation room and allowed those angry judgmental thoughts fueling my emotions to rise up to the surface. Then, using the Free Yourself process, I asked for each of those thoughts to be transformed. It literally took only a few minutes for me to reach a state of peace.

What actually took longer was getting over my resistance to using the Free Yourself process in the first place to let go of the feelings of anger and self-righteousness! Even after all these years of using this process and knowing how well it works, I still at times get seduced by those feelings, desiring to hang on to them as I revel in their false power. I also realized my feelings might be mirroring something going on in the man who had written the email.

About ten minutes after using the Free Yourself process, I felt at peace and was able to re-read his email from a place of non-judgment and love.

I responded the next day with the following email:

> *Dear Lee:*
>
> *Thank you for your email and for your heartfelt observations about my CarolHansenGrey.com site. I took your email into meditation with me this morning and asked for guidance.*
>
> *I do believe that "only love prevails" and practice its principle in my day-to-day life. However, I also believe we each have a responsibility to work in our own way toward making our*

world a better place, whether it be in areas that personally touch my heart (including raising spiritual awareness, promoting peace, facilitating health and healing, supporting truth and integrity in government, helping to empower the disempowered, safeguarding our environment) or in other areas just as important. One of the reasons I created my CarolHansenGrey.com site was to give me a space to share my work and my personal views on various topics.

That being said, I also know there are ways to share my views that are respectful rather than sarcastic. You did not specifically indicate on which page you found the "leftist propaganda garbage" so I took the time to carefully review the material on my site. I agree, some of the material I have posted in the political humor section and the political quotations section of the site is not respectful and I will be taking down the material that, in my opinion, fits that description.

Otherwise, I found only articles that were a meaningful representation of the concerns I have regarding the direction the current administration is leading this country and accurately reflect my point of view. I am sure your point of view is much different than mine and that does not mean you are wrong or I am wrong — it's simply a different perspective.

Most of us are aware of the political polarization in the U.S. (and throughout the world). My sense is there is actually more common ground between those who find themselves on the left or on the right of an issue than what appears on the surface. I believe if we were willing to start from that place of common ground we could begin to explore many ways to heal the polarization. I admit, however, sarcastic humor is not one of those ways. Thank you for giving me this opportunity to see an area in myself that is in need of healing.

*Thank you also, once again, for participating
in the World Peace Experiment. Together, no
matter what our political views, we will work
to co-create a world of peace where...*

Only Love Prevails, Carol

A few days later I received the following response:

*I really didn't expect a reply, seeing as how I live
in the "red" heartland and you live on the "left"
coast, but my heart was warmed as to how you
responded. You obviously do study the* Course in
Miracles *(I have on and off for two years now).*

*Since you were willing to re-evaluate some of the
text on your website, I felt that I had to do the same
(since I started this). It will be hard to get rid of a
whole section of Hillary humor (there is a lot of
funny stuff there, but it does create divisiveness).
I will also get rid of the political quotes section
showing the "less-than-fully-awake" statements
of Kerry, Gore, Dean, Pelosi, Harry, and the rest.*

*Einstein said that a problem cannot be solved at
the same level it was created. For years, I have
gotten really good at debating the polarizing issues
of the day. I've got the facts on my side, but the
problem with that is - you and many others have
a different set of facts from which to operate.*

*You are probably right about us having much
common ground and I am sorry that I came down so
hard on your personal web site. I guess it stemmed
from a seminar I went to the previous weekend, given
by Judith Pennington. She is a highly-evolved person
who occasionally lapsed into duality-consciousness
when talking about the president (I believe that Bush
43 is the most honest and straight-forward president
we have had in my lifetime). Anyway, I saw how
this highly-evolved person quickly came down into
the lower vibrations and brought me down also.*

My goal in life is to be able to rise above the chatter and really "know" the material in The Course in Miracles *and the other study group I attend - A.R.E (Association for Research and Enlightenment). Thank you for rising above my accusations and raising the bar for me to do the same.*

It is true that Only Love Prevails, Lee

This exchange helped me to see the importance of keeping the lines of communication open, even if the person is coming from a completely different viewpoint. I feel a positive connection with Lee now, whereas if I had chosen to simply ignore his email or, even worse, had responded in defensiveness or anger, a bridge to common ground would have never been built.

❧ TOOLS:

(9) Free Yourself from Fear Process *(p. 181)*
(11) Letting Go of Judgments Exercise *(p. 187)*
(13) Mirror Exercise *(p. 191)*

ELIMINATING SOURCES OF MEDIA NEGATIVITY

"You've got to accentuate the positive;
Eliminate the negative; Latch on to the affirmative;
Don't mess with Mister In-Between"
~Song lyrics by Johnny Mercer & Harold Arden

*T*his is a story of my journey in exploring ways to create a more peaceful environment, internally and externally. In 1991 I began by examining what I perceived to be the sources of negativity in my life and what became apparent to me was my attachment to keeping up with the daily news. Who among us has not fallen victim to the evaporation of a good mood simply by listening to the news?

As a result I took what some might consider a rather radical first step. I decided to eliminate watching television. This was a relatively easy task since the only thing I ever consistently watched was the late-night news after which I would go to bed filled with all the negativity I had just been fed by the media. Experiencing a good night's sleep was rare in those days and typically I would wake up grouchy and groggy.

So, it was rather startling to discover when I eliminated the late-night news from my routine, I began sleeping more soundly at night and waking up in a better mood.

What a revelation! Because the results of this simple experiment so impressed me, a couple of months later I decided to try another experiment. Could I further improve my mood if I stopped reading the newspaper? I decided to cancel my subscription and see what happened. A couple of weeks after my cancellation, I received a call from a newspaper sales representative who wanted to know why I had cancelled my subscription. I replied, "Because you never print any good news."

The sales rep responded rather incredulously, "Well, our job is to print the news."

"My point exactly," I said, "and it's rarely good news. I've decided I don't want to read about bad news."

After a brief hesitation, she persisted, "What can we do to get your business back?"

"I'll tell you what," I said. "The first time you print all good news just on the front page of the paper, you call me and I'll renew my subscription."

Well, this incident happened many years ago and I have yet to get a call, so I don't think they took my suggestion seriously. Nevertheless, I found by not listening to the news or reading the paper, I was actually feeling more energized and happy. And surprisingly, I did not feel as if I was missing out on anything important. After all, if something really big happened, my friends would be talking about it and I could get the news in that way without exposing myself to the negative media blitz.

About six months later I realized there was another source of media negativity I could easily eliminate. At 5:45 AM every morning I was awakened by music from my clock radio. However, if I did not get up right away, I would be treated to a newscast at six o'clock. One morning I lingered in bed long enough to hear the newscaster detail how many people had been killed in Oakland the night before. It was eight! I thought, "Good Grief! What am I doing to myself? I do not want to start off my day with this dose of media negativity!" So I tuned the clock radio to an all music station that did not report the news and from then on, I no longer exposed myself to any radio newscasts. I found each step in this journey to protect myself from media negativity, led me toward a more peaceful inner and outer life.

Sometime in 1994, three years after I had begun my news fast, I was standing in line at the grocery store when I heard the woman behind me complain, "I wish this line would hurry up. I have to get home. They're handing down a decision in fifteen minutes."

I turned to her and asked, "A decision?"

She stared at me like I had just dropped in from outer space and said, "O.J.!"

I simply replied, "Oh," and turned back toward the line in front of me. I had heard from friends about the infamous murder trial of O.J. Simpson but did not know, or care, about the details.

CHANGING YOUR CONSCIOUSNESS TO ACHIEVE WORLD PEACE

*"When you are inspired by some great purpose,
some extraordinary project, all your thoughts break their bonds:
Your mind transcends limitations, your consciousness expands
in every direction, and you find yourself in a new,
great, and wonderful world."*
~ Patañjali (as quoted by Wayne Dyer)

Every idea starts as a glimmer of inspiration. It was no different with the idea for the World Peace Experiment. Victor and I started meditating together every morning in 1995. For the first few years our daily meditations involved working with *A Course in Miracles* and following the lessons as a life path. It was an expansive and transformational experience. We came to understand there is really only love and everything else we experience is an illusion, something we make up in consciousness, individually and as a group.

In November of 1997 during one of our meditations I mused to Victor, "Wouldn't it be great if we could get enough people, critical mass, to let go of their thoughts about evil in the world and to shift their thoughts to a belief that there is really only love. If this could be accomplished, we could experience world peace in an instant."

Victor nodded in agreement and then asked the telling question: "How would we get enough people to do that?"

"I don't know," I responded. "But perhaps if we hold ourselves open to the possibility, we will be inspired with an idea."

In the meantime, Victor decided to research how many people represent critical mass. He went to the library and checked out books on quantum physics and other related topics and immersed himself in the study of what constitutes critical mass. What Victor gleaned from his research is that 80,000 people would create a critical mass. He explains it this way:

> "Physicists tell us that according to the laws of wave mechanics, the intensity of (any kind of) waves that are in phase with each other is the square of the sum of the waves. In other words, two waves added together are four times as intense as one wave, ten waves are one hundred times as intense, etc. Since thought is an energy, and all energy occurs as waves – we can surmise that 80,000 people all thinking the same thing together are as powerful, in terms of creating the reality that we all share, as the 6,400,000,000 people (80,000 times 80,000) who inhabit the planet, in their random chaotic thought. Therefore, 80,000 people all believing only in love, will be enough to change the planetary reality."

A couple of weeks later, during another meditation, the inspiration for what we have come to call the "World Peace Experiment" was born. The idea is to engage at least 80,000 people in a process that asks them to say the words, "Only Love Prevails," each time they personally perceive a negative event is happening, whether observing it in person or hearing about it from the media or other sources.

We believe this process will have the following effects:

* ❋ It will help participants stand in non-judgment and send positive energy to a perceived negative event.

* ❋ It will act as a barometer to help participants notice how much negativity they are personally perceiving.

* ❋ With practice and diligence it will help participants shift into a perception that only love prevails thus helping them achieve a state of inner peace.

* ❋ From that state of inner peace a ripple effect of positive energy will flow.

* ❋ As more and more participate, the ripple effect will expand and produce the desired effect — World Peace.

The following story illustrates the effects of this process.

A few years ago I received an email from a woman in California who asked to have her name taken off the World Peace Experiment list because she was not saying "only love prevails" much anymore. She therefore

FREEING YOURSELF FROM FEAR

World peace begins with inner peace.
What is reflected on the outer is merely a mirror
of what is on the inner.
As we begin to experience inner peace,
it will be reflected in our outer experience.
~ Carol Hansen Grey

According to *A Course in Miracles*, only **love** is real — fear is merely an illusion, something we made up. However in a time of global uncertainty and unrest, when fear appears to be everywhere, how do we keep ourselves centered in Love? How do we maintain our emotional and physical health and stay balanced? The most important thing we can do to dispel our fears is to acknowledge those fears and to transform them at the cause level.

Following are several stories illustrating how the Free Yourself process was used successfully as a personal practice as well as in a group setting to heal a variety of situations. My hope is you find these stories useful in understanding the power of the Free Yourself process and that they will ignite a creative spark within you to use the process to transform all thoughts that are limiting you from being the full, joyous, prosperous, healthy person you were meant to be.

✳ **Personal Practice Story 1:**
HEALING A PHYSICAL CONDITION

A woman who attended one of our workshops volunteered to be guided through the process on one issue creating a great deal of fear in her life. She was physically handicapped and walked very unsteadily to the front of the church with the use of canes. I began by asking her what issue she wished to work on. She said in a quiet voice, "Obviously, I am crippled and my condition is causing a lot of fear in my life." I said, "Are you willing to take the thought that you are crippled and turn it over to the Holy Spirit for transformation?" She said, "Yes."

"What is your next thought," I asked.

"I am in a lot of pain," she replied.

I directed her to say, "Holy Spirit transform the thought that I am in a lot of pain."

"What is your next thought?" I asked.

"I am getting weaker and weaker each day," was her answer.

Again prompting her, she said, "Holy Spirit transform the thought that I am getting weaker and weaker."

At this point I could feel an energy of skepticism coming from the audience as if they were saying, "Come on, get real... the woman is crippled..."

So I stopped the process for a moment to address the energy I was feeling. Turning to the audience I said, "I don't want any of you to think we are burying our heads in the sand. Obviously this woman has a handicap. We can all see it and she is living with it. However, she also has **thoughts** holding her handicap in place and **that** is the level we are working on."

The energy from the audience settled down and we continued for about another ten minutes until the woman reached some core thoughts: this was a congenital condition; her mother has it and is in a wheelchair; obviously, she will also end up in a wheelchair.

She asked the Holy Spirit to transform each of these thoughts.

I then said to her, "I believe you and I are complete at this point, but you've just begun your journey. Promise me you will go home and continue to allow every thought you have about your condition to come up into your consciousness and turn each one over for transformation. Then, please, contact me in about two weeks to let me know how you are doing."

About two weeks later I received a handwritten letter from this woman. In it she wrote, "Carol I have been crippled for 10 years and I have been a recluse for 10 years. I never go outside the house except to church on Sundays and to your workshop. I want you to know that I have now thrown away my canes. I no longer need them. And for the first time in 10 years, I have a social life. Thank you!"

❋ **Personal Practice Story 2:**
HEALING A FINANCIAL CONDITION

The next story illustrates how a woman used the *Free Yourself* process to heal her financial situation.

Victor and I were in Miami presenting a Lighten Up workshop. The minister had put us in a rather small classroom and was surprised when it filled to "standing room only." About five minutes after we began the workshop a woman and her 3-year-old son wedged themselves into the room. Someone in the audience, seeing them enter, got up and offered them a seat, right in the front row! I have to admit that I had some judgments about this woman bringing a small child to an evening workshop and of course, the child soon became bored and was running around the room.

At the end of the workshop we had a drawing for either a Lighten Up tape or a Free Yourself tape. To my surprise, the winner was the woman with the small child. Again, to my surprise, she chose the Free Yourself tape rather than the Lighten Up tape.

The next morning Victor and I were getting ready to check out of our motel when I received a phone call from the woman who had won the tape. She apologized for calling explaining I was the only person in the world who would understand the story she needed to tell me.

She told me she had seen a flyer for my workshop and knew she had to attend. She arranged for a baby sitter but at the last minute the sitter called and said she couldn't make it.

"I knew I had to go to this workshop," she said, "so I decided I would take my son with me. I went out to my car and found the battery was dead. So, in desperation, I borrowed my neighbor's car. On the way home from the workshop, I decided I wanted to buy a lottery ticket."

I could hear her take a deep breath before she continued. "Carol, you need to understand. I just lost my job and I didn't know how I was going to be able to put food on the table. So spending a dollar on a lottery ticket was a big deal! I asked my son to choose the numbers and then we went home. I went to bed listening to the Free Yourself tape and began transforming all my thoughts about my dire financial situation."

Another pregnant pause as I could hear her take a deep breath. "Carol, this morning I woke up and found out I have won $270,000 in the lottery!!"

I could hardly hold back my tears of joy for her and her son! Not only had this woman learned about the power of her thoughts, I had also learned a lesson about my judgments.

✤ Personal Practice Story 3:
SAVING A BUSINESS

This is the story of a woman who called me and asked if I thought the Free Yourself process could be used to help a failing business venture. She had invested all her money in opening a hair salon and day spa where she rented space to hair stylists and massage therapists. She was dismayed when those who had rented space from her were not working well together. Also, the business was not attracting the number of clients they needed to be profitable.

We scheduled weekly Free Yourself phone sessions over a period of several weeks to explore and transform all the limiting thoughts my client had around her business. We worked on several categories: thoughts centered around her financial investment and the risks she had taken; thoughts centered around the people she had attracted who were renting space from her and their inability to get along; thoughts centered around the numbers of clients her business was attracting; and thoughts centered around the financial success of her business.

As we worked through each category bringing up all the limiting thoughts and asking each to be transformed, her business began to transform. By the time we completed our work together, several of the old staff people had left the salon and she attracted a whole new group of people who worked well together creating a more harmonious environment. This, in turn, attracted new clients to her salon and the business became profitable.

✤ Group Process Story 1:
HEALING POST 9-11 FEAR

This first story happened in 2001 shortly after the attacks of September 11th. Everyone was in a state of shock from the events of that day and during one of our meditations I said to Victor, "You know, *The Course* says everything that is not love is fear. Right now so many people are in a state of fear in this country — fearing another attack and fearing the Anthrax problem. Also, there is a lot of hate in the world, which actually is the same energy as fear. I wonder if we could get some volunteers to do a group Free Yourself process to bring up all the fear thoughts they are feeling, and also to act as channels for all the other fear thoughts floating around in the group consciousness in our country.

I called our Unity Church and asked the minister what he thought about the idea. He was agreeable but said he didn't have an open slot until November 11th.

"Eleven-eleven," I said. *"Perfect!"*

So on November 11th about 60 people showed up to participate in a group Free Yourself session. Victor and I explained the process and told the audience we would work it "popcorn style." When anyone had a fear thought pop into their consciousness around the possibility of another attack, they would raise their hand. When I pointed to them, they would say their thought out-loud and the audience together would say "*Holy Spirit, transform that thought.*"

We started the process. For about 30 minutes the room was filled with fear thoughts being expressed and the Holy Spirit being invoked to transform the thoughts. Then I pointed to someone who expressed a positive thought. I stopped the audience and said, "Well, we don't want to have THAT thought transformed, so we will say "Holy Spirit, enhance that thought." For the next 15 minutes or so, we went back and forth between asking the Holy Spirit to transform and enhance the thoughts being expressed until all the thoughts were positive. Everyone in the room felt lifted up!

About two weeks later someone who had attended the group session came to me for a private appointment. When he arrived he said, "Well, you must really be proud of yourself."

"What do you mean?" I asked.

"Haven't you noticed?" he replied. "Ever since we did that process in the church there are no longer headlines in the paper warning of more terrorist attacks and the anthrax problem has gone away."

I told him I had **not** noticed because I don't read newspapers, but I sure was pleased we had done such great work together!

✳ Group Process Story 2:
HEALING A FINANCIAL CONDITION

This group process story involves an organization experiencing severe financial difficulties and considering
the need to close its doors. We gathered the twenty
members together and after explaining the process, I
led them through expressing their fear thoughts around
their own personal financial situations as well as their
thoughts around the financial situation of the organization. As each person in the group shared a deeply held
fear thought, we as a group asked the Holy Spirit to
transform the thought as it was being expressed. The
results were quite amazing. Many of the members
called me within a couple of weeks to tell me that their
personal financial situations had improved. The director
of the organization also called informing me the organization's finances had completely turned around.

✳ Group Process Story 3:
HEALING A PERSONAL PHYSICAL
CHALLENGE

This story is of a dear friend who in his forties had been
diagnosed with cancer of the throat. The prognosis was
dire in that the cancer had spread to his lymph glands.
Doctors were giving him about six months to live.

Shortly following his diagnosis, I did a group Free
Yourself session with him, his wife and two teenage children. I asked each of them to bring up all the fear and
anger thoughts they had around the cancer diagnosis.
At first it was difficult for them to verbalize the thoughts

they were feeling but once they got started, they came tumbling out in waves of anger, fear and grief. As each thought was expressed, we as a group asked the Holy Spirit to transform it. Toward the end of the process, positive thoughts began to emerge and as they were expressed we asked the Holy Spirit to enhance each one. We continued, alternating the process between asking for transformation and asking for enhancement, until there were only positive thoughts being expressed. As we ended the process, I instructed each of them to notice all fear thoughts that might arise in the future about this situation and to be diligent in immediately asking for those thoughts to be transformed.

Our friend went through chemotherapy as well as trying many alternative therapies. The good news is that today, more than five years later, he is healthy with no trace of cancer. In this case, the Free Yourself process worked beautifully alongside the other healing modalities he chose to use.

✽ Group Process Story 4:
HEALING A FAMILY MEMBER'S PHYSICAL CHALLENGE

This story involves the family of a dear friend who after surgery had slipped into a coma and was in the Intensive Care Unit. The family called and asked if I would come to the hospital and give her a Reiki treatment. They cleared it with the hospital staff and I started going to the hospital each day to give her Reiki. On the third day, I overheard the doctor talking with her husband and four adult daughters outside her room telling them it didn't look like she was going to make it. He suggested they start making arrangements to move her to a nursing facility and it might also be advisable for them to start looking into funeral arrangements.

After the doctor left, I asked the family if they would join me in the ICU waiting room. There, I told them, "Your mother is too weak right now to do what needs to be done to help herself through this challenge. She is depending on you. You need to be willing to look at all the thoughts you are now carrying that your mother is not going to make it through this challenge and turn them over to the Holy Spirit for transformation."

Right then and there in the hospital waiting room I led them through the Free Yourself process. The following day my friend regained consciousness. In three days she was moved out of ICU and a week later she was home from the hospital. That was over ten years ago. She is now in her eighties and still going strong today!

TOOL: (9) Free Yourself from Fear Process *(p. 181)*

DISSOLVING CLOUDS AND
DEVELOPING A LASER OF INTENT

*To fly as fast as thought, you must
begin by knowing that you have already arrived.
To bring anything into your life, imagine that it's already there.*

~Richard Bach, Author

Victor and I were sitting on a commuter train temporarily stopped while a problem on the track was being repaired. We were returning home from San Francisco where we had just held a meeting with an attorney. He had agreed to file corporation papers on our behalf for a new company we were forming with two other partners and told us it would take three to seven days to get the paperwork filed and back from the State. Because we had contracts to sign with another company in a couple of days, we needed the corporation papers completed within two to three days. The attorney said he would try but would not guarantee the paperwork could be expedited.

There we sat on the stalled train, Victor reading a book while I stared out the window. The day was bright and sunny with lots of wispy clouds forming intricate shapes in the otherwise clear, blue sky. I sat looking out the window remembering a book I had read many years ago called ***Illusions*** by Richard Bach. I smiled as I recalled his description of how his teacher taught him to dissolve clouds.

After reading that book I had become fascinated by the idea of dissolving clouds. In 1996 Victor and I took an eight-week road trip traveling from the West Coast to the East Coast and back again, presenting our workshop around the country. Eight weeks is a long time to be in a car so I decided this would be the perfect opportunity to begin honing my skills at dissolving clouds. I started by focusing on a small cloud and keeping it in my vision while thinking "dissolve, dissolve, dissolve…" To my amazement, the cloud would begin dissolving right before my eyes. The more I practiced the easier it got. Soon I was dissolving clouds on command without any effort whatsoever.

These memories made me smile and since I had nothing else to do while sitting on the stalled train, I decided to start dissolving some clouds. I had successfully dissolved about three clouds when I turned to Victor and said, "Well, I haven't lost my knack at dissolving clouds. I just dissolved three of them."

Peering over his reading glasses, he looked up from his book and said, "It sure would be great if you could figure out a way to put that skill of yours to practical use." We both laughed and he went back to reading.

I sat there thinking about what he had said. What **was** the energy that I was using to dissolve clouds? Could that energy be put to practical use and if so, how?

As I was pondering these and similar questions, the train began to move. As we sped by the countryside, I tried once again to focus on a cloud to dissolve. However, I found it impossible to do so. Because we were moving so fast, my field of vision was being broken up by the trees we were whizzing past. I could no longer focus on any one cloud. I closed my eyes and thought about the whole process of dissolving clouds. What did it entail? Focusing, without any distractions, all my energy and attention on **one** chosen cloud with a laser-like intent of thought — dissolve, dissolve, dissolve....

There must be a way to use that focused energy to produce a practical result. As I pondered it, a realization began to emerge. Dissolving clouds was actually a mani-festation technique that worked when there were no interrupting distractions. What if I were to use the same type of focused energy to create a picture of something I wished to manifest? Would that work?

As I have mentioned in other stories, since 1995 Victor and I have been meditating together every morning. The next morning I suggested we add a ritual to our meditation just before we say our prayers and go into our silent time. I proposed we decide between us to focus on one thing we both would like to manifest. Then during our silent time we would each hold our focused attention on a predetermined picture of the completed manifestation.

We had just been to the attorney the day before and the corporation papers were something we both wanted to manifest in an expeditious manner. So, we decided to focus on a picture of receiving an email from the attorney stating our papers had been filed and approved. The email would include an attachment of our filed and approved paperwork. We both could easily picture what it would look like to receive such an email.

We began our meditation holding the vision and focusing our energy for about three minutes on a mental picture of the email with the attachment. Completing our meditation, we continued our day as usual and both of us actually forgot about the manifestation process we had engaged in that morning.

At five o'clock that afternoon I checked my email and saw I had received an email from the attorney. The subject line read: "Articles of Incorporation" and I could see before I opened it that it included an attachment."

I clicked on the email and smiled when I read that our company had been successfully incorporated in the State of California. Attached were the State certified Articles of Incorporation.

The attorney had been able to get the corporation papers filed and approved by the State in less than one day!! Within nine hours of our meditation, we received the email exactly as we had envisioned it! Both Victor and I were in awe!

The following day we were facing a challenging meeting with an investor. We decided during our meditation to hold the picture of everyone at the conclusion of the meeting smiling and feeling happy to have reached a win-win for all concerned. I'm happy to report that the meeting turned out exactly as we had visualized. I also realized that I had found a practical use for my cloud dissolving skills! I encourage you to give it a try!

❧ TOOLS:

SENDING OUT LOVE SIGNALS:
THE DOLPHIN EXPERIENCE

The purest form of any "ripple"
is sharing God's unconditional love.
~Betty Eadie, Author

*W*hile on the phone with a customer who was inquiring about purchasing some Lighten Up products, I noticed he lived in Southern California. I mentioned to him that Victor and I were going to be in Southern California the following week to visit my daughter in Dana Point.

He immediately said, "Oh, if you're going to Dana Point, you need to experience the Dolphin Safari that goes out of the Dana Point harbor twice a day. The captain is so knowledgeable about Dolphins, you will not only get to experience the dolphins, but you will also learn all about them!"

This sounded like something I would truly enjoy, so Victor and I arranged with my daughter to bring her and her family along on this dolphin adventure. We were joined on the catamaran by another couple and their two grandchildren, ages ten and eleven, who had gone out the day before but had not seen any dolphins. It was the captain's policy to give you another excursion free of charge if you did not see any dolphins. The children had been rather disappointed by the previous day's outing and were really anxious to see dolphins on this trip.

We headed out of the harbor. What a glorious day! The temperature was in the 70s, the sun was bright, the sky was blue and the ocean was pristine, like a shimmering blue crystal. I was thoroughly enjoying myself just sitting back, soaking up the energy of the experience. I watched the two children standing at the front of the boat straining to see any sign of dolphins. We were about five miles out and still no sign of dolphins. The children were becoming discouraged.

The captain said, "Well, even if we don't see any dolphins, it really can't get much better than this." I had to admit it was peaceful and beautiful. But we **had** come to see dolphins, so I decided to try an experiment. Closing my eyes I went into a quiet meditation, consciously sending ripples of love radiating out from my heart as if I were dropping a stone into a pond.

With my eyes closed, I kept sending this love for about five minutes when I heard the captain exclaim, "There, look out there — there they are!"

Within minutes we were surrounded by literally hundreds of dolphins as far as the eye could see and some so close you felt you could reach out and touch them. They put on a great show, jumping and cavorting. It was simply amazing, and we all watched in a state of awe. The captain estimated we were seeing about

500 dolphins and said there were probably twice that number below the surface that we could not see. His astonishment was obvious as he shared with us that he had never seen so many dolphins on one of these outings. "We are experiencing a rare treat, indeed," he emphasized.

The dolphins stayed with us for about 45 minutes and as the boat turned to head back for shore, they also turned and led us back for about a mile before dispersing.

I felt truly blessed by their presence and the energy of the experience stayed with me for the rest of the day. This dolphin outing also helped me understand how we can attract truly magical experiences for ourselves and others by consciously sending out love signals.

 TOOL:

(5) Meditation Techniques *(p. 163)*

KEEPING A NEW YEAR'S JOURNAL

*Become aware that you already possess all the
inner wisdom, strength, and creativity you need
to make your dreams come true."
~Sarah Ban Breathnach, Author*

*I*n 1999 Victor and I decided we no longer
wanted to celebrate New Year's Eve by going
out and partying. We both felt it would be
much more enjoyable and meaningful for us to spend
New Year's Eve in a spiritual way.

So we decided to go to our meditation room around
nine o'clock in the evening, light the candles and talk
about the important things that had happened to us
during the year. The list started getting so long I suggested it would probably be a good idea to write it down
in a journal. Thus began our ritual of keeping a New
Year's Journal.

Each year during our New Year's Eve ritual, we list the
following items in our journal:

* all the family events (i.e., births, deaths, family
  reunions, etc.)

* all the new people we have met during the year
  and how they have made a difference in our lives

❋ all the trips we have taken and what was special about each one

❋ all the creative endeavors we have undertaken and how they have changed our lives

❋ all the things we have accomplished and why these things are important to us

We are **always** amazed at how long our list becomes and how very full our life has been during the year.

We then make a list of our goals for the new year. We start by looking back to the previous year's list of goals noting which ones we have accomplished; which ones we have decided to abandon; and which ones we will carry over to the new year. I remember the joy we felt one year when we found we had actually accomplished **all** the goals on our list. (*This doesn't happen often!*)

All of the above takes a couple of hours and we try to time it so that we can be done by midnight to ring our Tibetan bowl while we hold an intention for world peace. Keeping a New Year's journal has been a great way to keep a record of our activities and accomplishments. But more importantly, it is an inspirational tool that enables us to see how much we have grown personally and spiritually each year.

❋ **TOOLS:**
(5) Meditation Techniques (*p. 163*)
(24) The New Year's Journal Process (*p. 223*)

BEING AN ANONYMOUS DO-GOODER

No act of kindness, however small, is ever wasted.
- Aesop

This is a story of a tool I learned from a young college student who worked as an intern in my office at a local college. Several of us in the office were working late one evening to meet a deadline when this student looked at his watch and said, "Ohmygod! It's ten o'clock and I haven't done my good deed yet today." Heading for the door he called over his shoulder, "I'll be right back."

None of us knew what he was talking about, so when he returned a few minutes later, we were all curious to know about this "good deed" thing. He explained how his father had taught him to do an anonymous good deed every day and how he had been doing so since he was a young child.

"It can be anything, big or small," he said, "but the important thing to remember is your good deed must be done anonymously."

We asked the student if it wasn't sometimes difficult to "find" good deeds to perform. He said he was so attuned to looking for opportunities to do good deeds, he never had any problem finding them.

He went on to give us some examples of good deeds — picking up and properly disposing of litter, holding the door open for an elderly person, giving anonymously to a charity, dropping off magazines at a nursing home, helping a stranded motorist, shoveling the walk for a neighbor, calling the local municipal authorities to report a roadway hazard or, if possible, removing the hazard yourself. The key is to do the deed without letting anyone know you are doing it!

I asked him how he could do something for someone who was the recipient of his kindness without them knowing he was the one who had done the good deed. He smiled and said, "Well, you don't have to tell them your name. You just do the deed and if they insist on wanting to compensate you in some way, you simply tell them to "pay it forward." When we asked him what he had just done tonight, he smiled and said, "Well, if I told you, then it wouldn't be anonymous, would it?"

This incident happened many years ago and I've never forgotten the lesson this young man taught me. It was actually a version of the now famous mantra: "Practice random kindness and senseless acts of beauty." Since then I have not been as diligent about doing an anonymous good deed **every** day, but I do them often. I have found the mere act of doing something good for someone or for the planet without anyone knowing fills me with a child-like inner joy.

A Course in Miracles tells us, "the cost of giving is receiving." I have thus come to understand, whenever we give, we always experience a positive energy exchange. Giving is, therefore, the same as receiving — and the more we give, the more we receive.

This has been a powerful and life-changing idea for me. Just imagine the joy we could create in the world if everyone opened up to the harmonious continuum of giving and receiving.

 TOOL:

(25) Anonymous Do-Gooder Daily Ritual *(p. 225)*

He began by suggesting that I get in touch with my body. "Now," he said, "imagine her walking into this room right now. What does your body feel?"

Feeling a wave of nausea sweep over me, I said, "I feel like I am going to throw-up!"

We continued processing my feelings, uncovering all my thoughts lying deep beneath the emotional pain and turning them over to the Holy Spirit for transformation. Then I remembered the *"karmic debt release technique"* John had written about. I told Victor I would like to give it a try. I set my intention, inhaled deeply and said the following words slowly with a great deal of passion:

"I hereby release all karmic debt owed me: past, present and future — for all time! I release it NOW!"

I then exhaled as I outstretched my arms in release. I immediately felt waves of energy flowing outward from me. It seemed to fill the room and radiate out into the universe. It was one of the most powerful moments I have ever experienced!

Looking at me, Victor exclaimed, "You are absolutely glowing!"

We both sat in silence for several minutes savoring the energy. Then Victor once again suggested that I get in touch with my body and asked, "What if she walked into the room right now? What does your body feel?"

"Oh my God," I whispered. "I feel as if I could embrace her with love!"

About a week later I received a letter from this woman apologizing for the pain she had caused me and asking to be forgiven. The energy between us had been cleared.

I think of the karmic debt release technique as a dynamic forgiveness method that clears the negative emotional ties between people. These negative emotions sap our energy and keep us from fully experiencing unfettered joy.

Here is an analogy: You owe a dear friend some money but find yourself unable to repay your debt. You start avoiding your friend because you are feeling a great deal of guilt and emotional pain and thus your friendship suffers. Then one day your friend calls you and says, "I want to talk about our friendship and the debt we have between us. Your friendship is more valuable to me than any money that you owe me. I want you to know I have decided to wipe the slate clean — you no longer owe me any money. The debt is forgiven. All I ask for in return is your friendship."

How would you feel? How do you think it makes the person feel who did the forgiving? If it truly came from the heart, the feeling for both of you would be a release into love.

I like to imagine representatives from all the countries in the world coming together to do a Karmic Debt Release for all the perceived wrongs perpetrated throughout history. It would change the world!

TOOLS:

(9) Free Yourself from Fear Process *(p. 181)*
(23) Karmic Debt Release Process *(p. 221)*

FORMING A CO-CREATIVE RELATIONSHIP

*A co-creative relationship is one in which you are holding space
for answers to emerge through your intention,
faith, and gratitude.*
~ Ada Porat, Author & Holistic Health Practitioner

When Victor and I first got together as a couple in 1994, we were both committed to making our relationship a top priority in our lives. From the very beginning we had vowed to one another to always tell the truth and to create a space of safety for each other to be truthful. Each of us had been married before and acknowledged we were bringing to this relationship old baggage, as well as patterns of behavior, that had contributed to the demise of our previous relationships. We therefore were committed to letting go of the baggage and healing the patterns. We had what many would refer to as a "conscious relationship."

The first year we were together was challenging in many ways. We had to learn to trust one another and to feel safe in "telling the truth." Whenever one of our old patterns would rear its ugly head, we vowed to stop what we were doing, go to our meditation room and process it until we both felt the issue had been healed. The more we were willing to express our feelings and

STAYING BALANCED AND
LIVING IN THE PRESENT MOMENT

*The secret of health for both mind and body is not to mourn
for the past, worry about the future, or anticipate troubles,
but to live in the present moment wisely and earnestly.*

~Buddha

A powerful influence in my transformation process was the idea of living my life in the "present moment." I had often heard this was important, but did not really relate to the concept until a workshop I took illustrated what "living in the present moment" entailed. It means letting go of the past **and** letting go of the future — what a tall order!

During the workshop we were asked to think of our life's journey as if we were riding a horse. Most of us, we were told, are sitting backwards on the horse, holding onto a sack we are dragging behind the horse — a sack called the past. As we ride further and further through life, seemingly going forward but facing backward, we can easily become unbalanced as the sack grows larger and larger and begins to take up our entire field of vision. Our whole life's journey is being lived through our vision of the past. As a result, we may find it increasingly difficult to stay balanced as new challenges seem to come out of nowhere.

In order to live our life in the present moment and to gain a sense of balance, it is necessary to let go of that sack. We are then free to turn around on the horse and ride forward through life, facing and dealing with life's challenges as they appear.

Following the workshop, I was dozing off in bed one evening when I experienced an unusual vision. My mind began to run a movie of my life in reverse, starting from the present and replaying all my major life events until I was back in the womb. Then **poof**! I felt as if a bubble had popped and in that moment I knew that I had let go of my past. It was an amazingly powerful experience. The next morning I felt a sense of freedom and lightness I had never felt before.

Since that experience, I have consciously worked to keep my life balanced and to live as much as possible in the present moment. I do make plans and keep commitments. However, I think of my calendar as being engraved in sand, knowing plans can change on a moment's notice. Living in the now helps me be more understanding and accepting when life doesn't follow the path I had set forth. One of my favorite bumper stickers reads, "Life is what happens when we are making other plans." By consciously staying in the present moment, I can more readily adjust myself to life's unexpected surprises and maintain my sense of inner peace while enjoying the process.

TOOL: (20) Staying in the Now Exercise *(p. 213)*

EXPANDING TIME

*"The only reason for time is so that everything
doesn't happen at once."*
~Attributed to Albert Einstein

I was a member of a team of four women planning a large international event. Two of the
planners lived in Vancouver, BC, Canada, so it
was decided the two of us from California would fly to
Vancouver for a two-day, in-person planning session.

It took us a day just to get acquainted with one another
and to do a rough outline of what we wanted to accomplish with this event. The next day, the woman I'd trav-
eled with had to catch an early flight and we still had not
come up with a logistical plan. After she left, the three
of us made an outline of all the items we needed to
finalize and we came to the realization we could never
accomplish it all in the few hours we had remaining
before I had to catch my plane.

Instead of going into a panic or getting overwhelmed,
the three of us took an unusual approach. We went
into a fifteen-minute meditation and asked our angels
and guides to expand time to accommodate everything
we needed to accomplish. Coming out of the meditation, we set to work and what happened next was truly

magical. Within three hours we accomplished all the planning that in other circumstances would have easily taken a couple of days!

We even had time left for a walk on the beach before I had to catch my flight back to California!

This event changed the way I view and experience time. I no longer panic when I am met with what seems to be an impossible deadline. If it is something I truly need to accomplish in a short period, I simply take the time to reach a quiet state of inner peace and engage my angels to help me accomplish the task. They have never let me down!

 TOOL:

    (19) Engaging Your Angels to Expand Time *(p. 211)*

STORY 29

COUNTING YOUR BLESSINGS

"Faith is putting all your eggs in God's basket,
then counting your blessings before they hatch."
~ Ramona C. Carroll, Author

*W*henever I think about counting my blessings I'm reminded of the lyrics to a 1954 Irving Berlin song made popular by Bing Crosby: *"When I'm worried and I can't sleep, I count my blessings instead of sheep and I fall asleep counting my blessings."* More than just a song, however, this is actually sage advice. Many years ago I made a decision to put the song's advice to good use during my waking hours as well as when falling asleep at night. I use it to counteract the small frustrations in life like being stuck in traffic or temporarily losing my Internet connection, as well as for the major disappointments.

A very poignant example of how I used this process is when my father died several years ago. He and I had always been close and I thought of him as my best friend. He was in Wisconsin and I was in California making it impossible for us to see each other very often. Even so, we kept in touch through email several times a week and long phone conversations a couple times a month.

At 86 he became ill and had to be put into a nursing home. My step-mother called to tell me that he was declining rapidly, so I flew to Wisconsin to be with him. Everyday for the next week we spent hours together talking and reminiscing. During his final hours, I stayed by his side holding his hand and whispering in his ear. I told him how much I loved him and also told him it was okay for him to leave his body now and go into the light. I watched as his breathing slowed and he became more and more peaceful. I held his hand as he left his earthly body.

As we planned for his memorial, the sadness I felt was overwhelming. One of the things I did, however, to help me get through this very emotional time was to count my blessings. I began by counting the blessings involving my relationship with my father (i.e., the many years we had together, the love we had for one another, being able to be by his side as he made his transition) and then moved on to the overall blessings in my life (Victor by my side, a healthy body, a loving family). As I counted my blessings my feelings were lifted to a place of gratitude. My relationship with my Dad is one of my most treasured memories. When I think of him now, I immediately go into gratitude for the many blessings our relationship brought into my life.

Victor and I close our daily meditations by counting our blessings. Thus, we begin each day in a high state of gratitude. We find this helps us stay peaceful and balanced throughout the day.

TOOL: (15) Gratitude Exercise *(p. 197)*

FINDING THE GIFT IN EACH EXPERIENCE

*A bad day can help you glean wisdom you might
otherwise have overlooked or discounted.*

~Susun Weed, Author

Several years ago I decided to consciously look for the gift in each experience, even if there appeared to be none. As a direct result of this decision, there has been a perceptual shift in my reality. I have now come to believe everything happens in our lives ultimately for our highest good, even though at the time it may have the appearance of a "problem."

Prior to this shift, I would evaluate life events based on how my mind judged them (this was good, that was bad, etc.) often finding myself in a state of upset. Using this tool, I now go beyond the outer "appearance" to the inner meaning, always with the goal of finding the gift. Thus, I can now view what happens to me as a series of life-enhancing events I gift to myself. The following story is an illustrative example of the power of employing this tool.

Victor and I were on an eight-week cross-country road trip presenting our workshops. Somehow in the planning process, we had miscalculated our travel time between two final workshops on our schedule. We discovered we had to drive 900 miles in less than 24 hours.

We hit the road immediately following our second to last workshop and took turns driving through the night while the other slept. It was a grueling trip but we accomplished our goal — we arrived at our destination with 30 minutes to spare!

We were met by the minister who opened the church for us to set up and then left saying he had another appointment. We hurriedly set up for our workshop and waited. ***No one showed up!*** This had never happened to us and we were confused. We could have been angry and just packed up our stuff and gone back to our motel. However, we sat down and asked for the gift to be shown to us. Within a few of minutes of our "asking," the minister showed up and apologetically admitted he had forgotten to advertise the event in the church bulletin.

He then invited us to sit in on *A Course in Miracles* study group he was leading in an adjacent room. He offered to give us 15 minutes toward the end of the meeting to introduce ourselves and tell the group about our work. Our workshop typically ran two to three hours, so we didn't think 15 minutes would give us enough time to actually give an adequate presentation. However, we accepted his invitation.

Because Victor and I are students of *The Course*, we felt comfortable and "at home" joining the study group. As members of the group read from *The Course* and discussed it, we found it easy to immerse ourselves in the energy of love. As promised, toward the end of the meeting the minister introduced us, briefly explaining the scheduling mix-up. Surprisingly, we found it easy to present our material to the group in the 15-minute time-frame.

The gift we were given was profound. We ended up selling more books and tapes in that one evening than we had sold at any of our other workshops. In addition, the minister was so impressed with our impromptu presentation he became our advocate, ordering all our products for the church bookstore and promoting our work. If we had presented the workshop as planned, the minister would not have attended because of his *Course in Miracles* study group commitment and no connection would have been made. We would have just been another couple who had presented a workshop at this church.

✖ TOOLS:

(5) Meditation Techniques *(p. 163)*
(26) Finding the Gift Prayer *(p. 227)*

Part 2

The Tools

TOOL 1
CREATIVE WAYS TO ADD SILENCE
TO YOUR LIFE

Because our world is inundated with sound and noise, it has become an increasing challenge to experience true silence. You might be able to find it by taking a walk in the woods and, if you have the time and opportunity to do that, you certainly have a built-in advantage. But not everyone has access to a quiet woods or the time to get away.

So, I have found it helpful to create silent times during my everyday activities, thereby opening myself up to my inner creative voice — a voice easily heard when I consciously create the environment.

One of my favorites is to create silent time while driving in my car. Instead of turning on the radio or listening to music, I drive in silence. I have also made the conscious decision to work in silence at my computer. In the past I often listened to music. Now, in that silent space, I find my creativity blossoms and my productivity soars.

I have become so accustomed to enjoying many hours of silence a day, it is hard for me to imagine how I could have functioned any other way.

Following are some suggestions for adding silence to your life:

Turn off the radio or television when you are working. Many people keep this background noise going all the time and if you are one of those people, you might be amazed after a short period of time how much more you can get accomplished when you work in silence. This is especially true of any work requiring mental concentration. It may take a short while for you to feel comfortable doing this, but try to stick with it for at least two weeks to give yourself a chance to get used to it. If your workplace is a naturally noisy environment, you might consider getting a noise-canceling headset, if appropriate.

At home, create a space where you can go to be undisturbed. This may be a bedroom, a bathroom, a sun porch or even a walk-in closet. Make a "Do Not Disturb" or a "Quiet" sign to hang on the door. Let your family know that when the sign is posted, you are in need of some silent time and want them to honor it. In your space, take time for some deep breathing and enjoyment of the silence. Try to visit your "Silent Space" at least once a day. It may become the most enjoyable part of your day!

In the car, when possible, drive in silence without listening to the radio or to music. This is difficult when you have a car full of kids, but there are usually times when you are driving alone (i.e., on your way to pick up the kids from school, running errands when the kids are in school or when the baby is asleep in the car, commuting to work, etc.). This is a good way to take advantage of that alone time to add some silence to your life.

Consider going on a "silent retreat." These retreats are sponsored by many different churches and organizations and usually involve a group of people who have made the commitment not to speak to one another for the duration of the retreat. In addition, no outside sounds are allowed (other than the sounds of nature) to intrude on the silence (i.e., no music, television, radios, etc.) The point is to be able to get in touch with your thoughts on a deep level as you focus your attention inward.

If you cannot find an organized silent retreat, consider creating one of your own. Go somewhere for a day (or a few days) where you can be alone in a quiet environment. Bring a notebook and pens or pencils, so you can jot down any thoughts that come to mind during your silence. You will be surprised at how renewed you will feel and you may actually find it to be a life-changing exercise!

TOOL 2

FIND YOUR JOY EXERCISE

"When you are looking for the work that you came to this planet to do, meditate on what brings you joy, crystallize that in your heart, and build your work around it."

~ Matthew Fox, Theologian

To begin this exercise, find a quiet, comfortable place where you can be undisturbed for twenty to thirty minutes. Have a notebook and pen or pencil handy. Light a candle and take a few deep breaths as you relax into your chair. With your eyes closed, ask yourself the following question:

"If I did not need to be concerned about supporting myself, what service could I do to make the planet a better place while at the same time, make my heart sing?"

Be with that question in the silence of your meditative space. As thoughts begin to filter in, write them down in your notebook. At first the thoughts may seem irrelevant to the question, but write them down anyway.

It may take several meditative sessions to get to your answer, but you will know it when it comes because it will repeat itself in several forms. If you have been keeping your notebook, you will be able to document this and find the emerging answer.

For some the answer comes as a clear career path. For others, the answer may simply be a word such as "empowerment" or "healing" or "travel." It is then important for you to meditate each day on the word that has come through asking to be shown ways to incorporate it into your work.

For me the word "empowerment" came through and over the years I have been given many ways of serving the planet through my own personal empowerment and by helping others empower themselves.

* I began my journey of spiritual awakening by running a healing center where empowerment became a central theme in my own healing process as well as in my work with the center's practitioners and clients.

* When I was running my Macintosh consulting business, I helped my clients empower themselves on their computers.

* Through my workshops and my Open Heart Press books and CDs I help my clients empower themselves by learning to love themselves and freeing themselves from fear

* Through my web design business I help my clients empower themselves through their websites.

In every area of my work, empowerment plays a key role in the service I provide, and this truly makes my heart sing!

TOOL 3
SUBCONSCIOUS HEALER EXERCISE

*I*n this exercise your goal is to communicate with your subconscious healer who resides within you, who knows everything about you, and who is there to do your bidding. Begin by giving your subconscious healer a name to help you personify it.

Then acknowledge to your subconscious that it knows everything about your body and therefore knows what is causing a particular ailment. Lastly, give it an order to heal the ailment. Issue this order out loud three times.

It is important to talk with your subconscious healer out loud (instead of just thinking). You don't need to talk loudly (you can whisper), but it is important for your words to be heard by your ears and processed by your brain's auditory system. Your subconscious then receives the message on an entirely different level than if you simply "think" your request.

So, use this process whenever you have a specific issue that you need to heal. For example, if you have a headache, say three times to your subconscious healer, "You know everything about my body. You know how to

As a reflection of how our lives are continually changing and evolving, our altars also change over time. We find we are often guided to give away a sacred altar object to a friend, thus making room for a new item on our altar. Let your altar be a reflection of you, changing as you change.

❊ USING FENG SHUI IN CREATING YOUR SACRED SPACE

We endeavored to keep the principles of Feng Shui in mind when placing items in our sacred space. Thus in our "wealth area" we hung a butterfly mobile that is constantly in motion, in our "children area" we hung a photo collage of our children and grandchildren, in our "helpful people" area is our Quan Yin statue and painting of Jesus, in our "partnership area" we hung a "dancing helix" with rainbow colored crystals. We placed our bookcase in our "knowledge" area and our "family area" is where we have placed our world map and peace altar. Our "fame area" is a window and above it we hung a sun catcher. Our "career area" is the door where we enter our sacred space and above the door we hung a round rose quartz crystal. The "health area" is in the center of the room and there we have a Tibetan bowl that we ring each morning to begin and end our meditation.

For more information about Feng Shui, check the Resources Section on the SimpleHealingTools.com website.

MEDITATION TECHNIQUES

*"We could say that meditation doesn't have a reason or doesn't
have a purpose. In this respect it's unlike almost all other things
we do except perhaps making music and dancing.
When we make music we don't do it in order to reach
a certain point, such as the end of the composition.
If that were the purpose of music then obviously
the fastest players would be the best.
Also, when we are dancing we are not aiming to arrive
at a particular place on the floor as in a journey.
When we dance, the journey itself is the point,
as when we play music the playing itself is the point.
And exactly the same thing is true in meditation.
Meditation is the discovery that the point of life is always
arrived at in the immediate moment."*

~Alan Watts, Philosopher (1915-1973)

Meditation can take as many forms as there are individuals on earth. Some people find quiet music playing in the background helps them reach a meditative state. Others prefer silence. There is no right or wrong way to meditate. What I share with you on the following pages are simply some forms of meditation I have found useful to help me arrive at "the immediate moment," as Alan Watts describes in the above quote.

❋ Basic Meditation - Quieting the Mind

Sit in a comfortable position on the floor or in a chair. Let your eyes focus on a particular object. I like to focus on something that plays with light such as a candle or a crystal, but it really could be anything. As you focus, start to notice the in and out rhythm of your breathing. Consciously slow your breathing by taking deeper, longer breaths. Sometimes counting helps – slowly count to three as you inhale, hold for a count of three and then exhale to a count to three. Imagine with each inhaled breath, your body is being filled with light. Imagine with each exhaled breath, your body is releasing stress and tension, becoming more and more at ease.

As you reach a relaxed state, you may decide to close your eyes to more fully engage with your inner self. Allow yourself to notice any thoughts infiltrating your awareness. Imagine these thoughts dissolving into the light and leaving with each breath until you have reached a place of "no thought," a place of emptiness, a place of quiet and inner peace. This is a place of rejuvenation — stay in this place as long as you wish.

❋ Ending Your Meditation

When you wish to end your meditation, do so by opening your eyes and slowly bringing your consciousness back to where you are in the room. Look around the room, noticing your surroundings. Tilt your head from side to side as if you were loosening up a stiff neck. Bring your breathing back to normal. Move your shoulders and stretch your arms. I like to end my meditation in gratitude by saying "Thank You!"

Dancing Meditation

Turn on a recording of some favorite meditative music. With the music in the background, quiet your mind as described in the Basic Meditation above. When you've reached a relaxed state, stand up and slowly begin to sway to the music. Imagine the music moving through your body. Imagine your body melding into the music. Let the music direct the movements of your body. Continue your meditative dance for as long as is comfortable. When you are ready to come out of your meditation, do so by slowly bringing your consciousness back into the room. Open your eyes and take a few deep breaths.

Kything Meditation

Wikipedia describes Kything as deriving from an old Scottish word, "kythe" meaning, "to make visible." It is a "wordless, mind-to-mind communication in which one person, in essence, almost becomes another, seeing through their eyes and feeling through their senses. The idea may be based on the concept of Oneness, which states that all that exists, is one in its source and end."

I learned this specific meditation technique years ago and find it useful when I want to understand and/or heal a relationship. I also use it to simply reach a feeling of Oneness with the Divine.

To begin your Kything Meditation, sit in a comfortable position, quieting your mind as described in Basic Meditation. Once you have reached a state of "no thought," visualize in your mind's eye a triangle as shown below.

KYTHING MEDITATION

I am present
for God
2

1
I am present
for myself

3
I am present for
my special intention

Focus on the bottom left corner of the triangle and state silently to yourself, "I am present for myself." Stay focused on being present for yourself until you feel completely centered.

Taking a deep breath, move your mind's eye to the top of the triangle and again state silently to yourself, "I am present for ... *(here you insert whatever word you are comfortable using to represent God/Goddess, Supreme Being, Divine Light, etc.).* You can stay in this state for as long as you wish. Indeed, I often stay in this state without moving to the third state, simply because it is a wonderful way to reach a feeling of Oneness with the Divine.

If you choose to move to the next level, focus your mind's eye on the lower right corner of the triangle and state silently to yourself, "I am present for ... *(here you insert the name of the person with whom you wish to connect).* In this state, you can say the words of love and forgiveness that you may have been unable to communicate in person. Stay in this state until you feel complete and at peace.

Bring yourself out of your meditation using the process described in Basic Meditation, knowing that a healing has begun.

TOOL 6

THE NEWS FAST

*By taking a news fast, you can develop a more conscious
relationship with the media – and promote greater
mental calm within yourself.
When you spend more time in harmonious mental states,
your body will function better, and anxiety and
over-stimulation may be minimized.*

~ Dr. Andrew Weil

I took what some may consider to be radical
steps when it came to eliminating the negativity of media news from my life. I began by
first eliminating my television viewing, then later by
canceling my newspaper and finally by turning off my
radio. All this began as an experiment and happened
over a span of several months in 1991. During that time
I noticed I was actually feeling happier as well as more
calm and centered.

Some time after I did my successful personal experiment, I heard about a "news fast" idea being promoted
by Dr. Andrew Weil. He suggested that avoiding the
news for a few days or a week might help renew your
spirits. He made his case by citing statistics indicating
news shows had actually increased their emphasis on
crime even though crime rates nationally were on the

decline. He also stated that studies show negative news stories can provoke changes in mood, creating feelings of anxiety, sadness and depression.

I think the idea of going on a news fast is an efficient and effective way of helping you recognize and understand the negative impact watching and reading media news has on your life. I encourage you to make a commitment to give up the news for a week and then assess how you feel. You might decide, as I did, to give it up completely!

TOOL 7
ONLY LOVE PREVAILS EXERCISE

*V*ictor and I, through our own shift in consciousness, have come to believe we are all one mind. We therefore feel if enough people could shift their own personal perception—change their minds—about the existence of evil, then the whole planet could shift into a perception of love.

We have also come to believe that world peace begins with each individual achieving a state of peace within themselves. One way we can begin to do that for ourselves is to become aware of the "negative" influences in our lives and choose consciously to eliminate or shift those influences.

In **Tool 6,** I offered ways to recognize and eliminate the negative influences of the media. The following two-step exercise focuses on helping you to personally achieve a state of inner peace. As more and more of us become peaceful within, the ripple effect will be a more peaceful world.

STEP ONE

Say the words, ***"only love prevails,"*** whenever you perceive a negative event is occurring. This phrase sends "positive" energy to the perceived negative event as you stand as an observer in non-judgment. Saying these words will also help shift the underlying perception that for good to exist, evil must also exist (polarity theory).

As your perception shifts, you will perceive less and less negativity. This step of the process therefore acts as a barometer to help you measure your own sense of inner peace. The less negativity you perceive, the less you will find yourself needing to affirm, **"only love prevails."**

✳ STEP TWO

Become aware of the profound impact the news media has on your perception. As explained in **Tool 6**, do whatever you need to do to protect yourself from exposure to "negative" or fear-based stories in the media. This may mean giving up watching or listening to newscasts or reading newspapers, or it may mean that you simply filter your exposure to the news media and become very selective about what you do listen to, read or watch. Just bringing your awareness to the negativity that permeates the news media will help create a shift in your consciousness.

In the late 1990's I read an interesting article. It stated that while the murder rate had actually gone down by twenty percent in the U.S. over the previous year, the media reporting of those crimes had increased a whopping 600%! If we depend only on the media as our benchmark of what is happening on our planet, it would be easy for us to believe only evil exists.

The truth is, the reports of so-called negative occur-
rences that permeate newscasts are, in most cases,
isolated incidences. Most of what happens on this planet
falls into the "good news" area. However, because so
many of us have become addicted to the diet of negative news fed us by the media, positive news stories are
rarely reported.

Victor and I believe the consciousness of the planet
could shift if enough people: 1) stopped exposing themselves to the negative energy generated by the news
media, and 2) said the words "only love prevails" whenever they were exposed to a report of a perceived
"negative" event. This, we feel, would be a giant step
toward individuals achieving a state of inner peace.
When critical mass is reached where enough people
are peaceful within, the ripple effect will be a peaceful
world.

TOOL 8
LIGHTEN UP PROCESS

*L*ighten Up is a two-step process. Once you've completed the first step you never have to repeat it. From there on, simply do the second step every day.

☀ STEP ONE: Mirror Exercise

To begin the Lighten Up process stand naked in front of a mirror, really look at your body and say *"I love you"* out-loud to each part of your body. This step is important because it opens a window in your mind – one that may have been closed for years – to the idea that your body is lovable no matter its shape, its state of health, or how you may have abused it. **Your body is lovable**.

As I mentioned above, you need only do this one time—to start off the process.

☀ STEP TWO: Your 5-Minute-A-Day Nurturing Process

Each day after you shower or bathe, honor and nurture your entire body by moisturizing it. As you moisturize,

TOOL 9
FREE YOURSELF FROM FEAR PROCESS

A *Course in Miracles* teaches that only love is real. It tells us that fear is merely an illusion, something we made up. Yet, how do we keep ourselves centered in love? How do we bring ourselves to a place of inner peace? How do we, as spiritually conscious people, acknowledging our oneness with all life, open our hearts to embrace without judgment those who are filled with anger?

The Free Yourself from Fear process is a tool that transforms fear because it works at our thought level — the cause level of all our emotions. Victor and I have been successfully using this process in our own lives and with clients for many years. The results are always amazing.

THE PROCESS

* **STEP 1**: Identify an area or situation where you are feeling limited, angry, frustrated or fearful. This can be centered around your finances, your job, your goals, your relationships, your family — anything upsetting to you.

✸ **STEP 2**: Identify a spiritual partner with whom you wish to work. It could be Holy Spirit, Jesus, Buddha, a Guardian Angel, Divine Presence — any spiritual entity with whom you feel a comfortable connection. The important part in choosing your spiritual partner is that you can actually visualize this spiritual being as a real entity.

✸ **STEP 3**: Find a quiet, comfortable place where you can be undisturbed. Take a series of deep, relaxing breaths. Then think of the situation you have chosen to address. Allow your very first thought about the situation to filter into your consciousness. It may take a little while to actually identify a first thought — you have probably kept them hidden or buried for quite some time, afraid to let them show themselves to you. That is normal. Simply keep thinking about the situation and paying attention to any thoughts that arise. As a thought rises to the surface, ask your spiritual partner to transform the thought. *(For example, "Holy Spirit, transform the thought that I have no choice in this situation.")* Then move to the next thought, again asking that it be transformed. (Note: This can be done silently; it is not necessary for you to ask out loud.)

Soon the thoughts will begin to surface rapidly. You may start feeling overwhelmed. Continue to breathe remembering that your only job in this process is to identify and turn the limiting thoughts over to your spiritual partner for transformation. You do not need to do the work of transformation or figure out how it will be done — that is the task being done by your spiritual partner.

Continue Step 3 until you notice that interspersed with the limiting thoughts, positive thoughts are beginning to emerge in your consciousness around the situation. As these thoughts emerge, ask your spiritual partner to **enhance** those thoughts. You will find that as the limiting thoughts have been turned over for transformation, your consciousness will be filled more and more with positive thoughts.

STEP 4: If you feel you are stuck and can't seem to pull up the limiting thoughts that you know are deep within, you can say the following prayer. Please substitute "Holy Spirit" with the spiritual partner you have chosen:

"Holy Spirit, shine your light of truth on this situation. Enable me to identify the thoughts that are limiting me from being my full expression of love and to turn them over to you for transformation."

Breathe deeply after saying the prayer and allow your thoughts once again to focus on the situation you have chosen to address.

✤ **STEP 5**: When you have turned over all limiting thoughts and you feel complete, end with a prayer of gratitude thanking your spiritual partner for working with you. It can be as simple as the one below:

"Holy Spirit, thank you for being my partner in this sacred, healing work."

❈ ONGOING WORK

Once you have completed the above process, your continuing work is to notice throughout the day when a limiting thought enters your consciousness. Immediately call on your spiritual partner and say, "Transform that thought." Make this a habit.

❈ WORKING WITH A BUDDY

This process is particularly effective when you have engaged the cooperation of someone you trust — such as a spouse, a relative, a close friend, a business partner. Explain the process to them and ask them to let you know if and when they notice that you've made a limiting remark in the course of any conversation. Give them permission to say to you, "That's a thought that could be transformed!"

Engaging in this process with a trusted person who has your permission to point these things out to you, can be helpful in more rapidly freeing you from the fear that has kept you from your goal of achieving inner peace and living in the energy of love.

TOOL 10

RAINBOW CLEARING PROCESS

*T*his two-step process can be used to clear yourself of energy that is not your own. I use it after a session with a client so that I am clear for my next client. I use it whenever I have been in a large gathering, whenever I feel an emotion that seems to come "out of the blue" or whenever I feel tired for no apparent reason.

The purpose of the process is to get yourself back into your own energy. Anyone who works with the public *(i.e., a bartender, a beautician, a receptionist, a teacher, a banker, a retail clerk, a cashier, a nurse, a doctor, a therapist, a healer)* naturally takes on energy from others. It is, therefore, important to have an easy and effective way to clear out energy that is not your own. This is a very simple process that takes just seconds to do.

* **STEP 1:** Close your eyes and visualize a rainbow colored shaft of light coming out of the sky into the top of your head. Now, in your mind's eye, see that rainbow light spreading throughout your body, filling every cell with rainbow light. Feel it filling your head and moving down through your neck and shoulders, down your arms and out

your finger tips. Feel it filling your chest, stomach and abdomen and all your internal organs. Feel it moving down into your hips, legs and feet until rainbow light is coming out of your toes. Your whole body is now radiating rainbow light. See it! Feel it! (This may take a minute or two in the beginning to visualize, but as your body gets acquainted with the process, soon it will take only a few seconds to fill yourself with rainbow light.)

✷ **STEP 2:** Choose for yourself a symbol of safety and protection — a safety shield — and surround yourself with it. Your symbolic shield can be anything — a powerful animal, an angel, a geometrical shape such as a pyramid or a sphere — any symbol that represents to you safety and protection.

See yourself inside your symbol — it is all around you. With your shield in place, you are now protected from taking on energy that is not yours.

TOOL 11

LETTING GO OF JUDGMENTS EXERCISE

*T*his is an interesting exercise that helps you develop a sense of how much you judge others (and yourself), perhaps without even being aware of it, and also helps you to let go of those judgments. Why is this important? When we judge others we feel separate from them and our hearts become closed to love. If one of the goals in life is to reach a state of inner peace where "only love prevails," then one of the first steps is to let go of our judgments. Commit to doing this exercise every day for a week.

* **Step 1:** Get a little pocket-sized notebook and a small pencil or pen that you can easily carry with you.

* **Step 2:** Write the date that you start the exercise on the first page.

* **Step 3:** Every time you notice yourself making a judgment say to yourself, "I choose to release myself from this judgment" and then make a tick-mark in the notebook.

For ease of counting at the end of the day, keep track of them in multiples of five as shown below:

* **Step 4:** At the end of the day, tally up your tick marks and write the total on the bottom of the page.

* **Step 5:** Repeat steps 2 through 4 every day for a week.

This exercise, if done diligently, usually produces interesting results. Most of us do not pay attention to our judgments — after all, many of them are thoughts we have carried with us since childhood. These thoughts have shaped our perception of who we are and what we believe. So, by keeping track of our judgments in this non-judgmental way, the number we make each day may be surprising.

Once we become conscious of our judgments and choose to release them, we free ourselves from them. Thus, we can open ourselves up to thinking and behaving in a more loving way.

TOOL 12
EMOTIONAL RELEASE EXERCISE

*O*ften when we perceive someone has wronged us in some way *(i.e., insulted us, humiliated us, told lies about us, cheated us)*, it can be difficult to keep from getting wrapped up in a spiraling energy of anger. What they said or did can swirl around our consciousness and permeate our thoughts, knocking us off-center and making us lose our sense of balance. These angry thoughts can become a consuming energy, keeping us awake at night and negatively affecting our work, our family life and our sense of well-being.

Whenever you find yourself caught in this state of mind, try the following exercise. It is actually in the form of a prayer and I have found it extremely helpful whenever I get stuck in a negative spiral of anger.

> *Holy Spirit, I ask to be released from this feeling of anger. Shine your light of truth on my relationship with [insert name here]. Dispel all my illusions and bring me to a state of peace.*

Say the prayer three times, slowly, taking deep, cleansing breaths between each repetition.

This may simply be enough to enable you to break free of your anger thoughts. If the anger, however, continues to grip you, move to the Free Yourself from Fear Process (Tool 9, page 181) asking the Holy Spirit to transform your thoughts about the person who has caused your upset. You can also use the Kything Meditation (found in Tool 5, page 165).

TOOL 13
MIRROR EXERCISE

*W*hen, for no apparent reason, you start feeling angry or uncomfortable around someone in your life, they may be mirroring something within you that needs healing. Several tools described in this book can help you overcome these feelings, including: the Free Yourself Process (Tool 9), the Rainbow Clearing Exercise (Tool 10), the Emotional Release Exercise (Tool 12), and the Kything Meditation (Tool 5). This is another exercise to help you uncover what might be going on and to bring yourself to a state of inner peace.

Step 1: Go into a quiet space and take a few deep cleansing breaths, feeling yourself relax with each breath.

Step 2: Say the following prayer:

> *"Holy Spirit, shine your light of truth on my relationship with [insert name]. Show me how this relationship serves as a mirror revealing areas within myself that need healing. Help me heal those areas and reach a state of inner peace."*

Step 3: After saying the above prayer, take a few more cleansing breaths, opening yourself up to any insights that come through in this meditative state. If anger thoughts come up, use the Free Yourself process to transform them.

In my willingness to use the mirror exercise, I am soon given the insights I need to heal myself and to shift into a space of gratitude and love for the person who had held up the mirror!

TOOL 14

LAW OF ATTRACTION EXERCISE

*T*his is the process I used to attract Victor into my life. It originally came from an Abraham-Hicks tape I was given years ago.

Supplies needed: A notebook and a pen or pencil.

* **STEP 1**: Decide what it is you want to manifest. This exercise works best when you focus on one goal at a time, so decide what your goal will be and focus only on it. Once you have successfully manifested it, you can use the process again to manifest your next goal.

* **STEP 2**: Set aside twenty minutes each day to go into your "manifesting workshop." Sit in a comfortable position and take a couple of deep cleansing breaths.

* **STEP 3**: In your notebook write the date and an affirming statement of what it is you want to attract. For me it was a relationship, so I wrote, "I want to attract a loving man into my life."

* **STEP 4**: Next, list all the positive criteria you want to incorporate into your beginning statement. Avoid negative statements *(i.e., I don't want an abusive man)*. Instead always write

positive statements *(i.e., I want a man who is loving and caring.)*

For example, my list began like this:

- » I want a man who is caring
- » I want a man who is strong, yet nurturing
- » I want a man who is on a similar spiritual path
- » I want a man who respects who I am
- » I want a man who honors my work
- » I want a man who will work alongside me

✽ **STEP 5**: Throughout the day, notice what begins to show up in your life and use that to refine your list. For instance, using my example of wanting to attract a loving man into my life, if you find men start showing up in your life who meet the qualities on your list except they are perhaps all too young or too old, use that information to refine your list.

- » I want a man who is my age, or
- » I want a man who is between the ages of ___ and ____

Also, throughout the day notice the qualities of other people in relationship and add the qualities you most admire to your list.

Another example of when you might use this process is if you are looking for a new job. Your list may start out something like this:

- » I want to find a new job easily and effortlessly.

» I want a job where my skills and talents are honored and appreciated.
» I want a job that will enable me to support myself and my family comfortably.
» I want a job that helps me to expand my skills.
» I want a job that is interesting.
» I want a job where I enjoy and respect the people I work with.

Keep adding to and refining your list each day as you notice what shows up in your life. For instance, if you get a job offer that meets most of the requirements on your list but it is a really long commute, you might add:

» I want a job with a short, easy commute.

Using another example, perhaps you want to sell your house at a time when there are tons of houses on the market and none are selling. Using the law of attraction exercise as described above, make a list of exactly what you would like to see happen.

For example, your list could look something like the following:

» I want to attract the right and perfect buyer for my house
» I want the buyer to love the house
» I want the buyer to have the financial ability to buy the house
» I want the sale to go through easily and effortlessly
» I want everyone involved in the transaction to feel satisfied with the deal

As mentioned earlier, it is important to keep adding to and refining your list each day as you notice what is showing up. For instance, if a potential buyer shows up but wants you to make costly improvements before signing the deal, improvements you are not willing to make, then you want to add to your list something like the following:

> » I want a buyer who loves the house just the way it is
> » I want a buyer who appreciates the value this house represents
> » I want the buyer to feel good about the price of the house

Remember, your list is not static — it will change and evolve as you become more and more precise. This process helps you become clear about what you really want to attract. The clearer and more specific you are, the more easily the universe sends you exactly what you want!

TOOL 15
GRATITUDE EXERCISE

*L*et this exercise become a habit. You can start by verbally (or mentally) listing everything you can think of for which you are grateful. Do this every time you find yourself disappointed or upset throughout the day. By listing things in your life for which you are thankful, you attract to yourself the energy of gratitude which immediately helps dissipate the energy of anger or disappointment.

In *Story 29: Counting Your Blessings*, I related how you can use this exercise to help in big issues (such as the passing of a loved one). It is also an effective way to let go of minor everyday irritations. As an example, I used this process one day when I was driving to meet a client. Someone cut me off on the freeway and almost caused an accident. Shaken, my mind filled with angry thoughts as I watched the driver who had cut me off continue to recklessly weave in and out of traffic at a high speed. Not wanting to stay in an agitated frame of mind, I remembered I could use the gratitude exercise to shift my emotional state. I immediately started to mentally list things for which I was grateful:

* I am so grateful I wasn't involved in an accident

* I am grateful for my loving family

197

* ❧ I am grateful for my health

* ❧ I am grateful for my friends

* ❧ I am grateful for my car ...

Within a few minutes by tense body relaxed and I found my anger had been replaced by a feeling of gratitude and love. If I had not used the gratitude exercise in this instance, I probably would have arrived at my appointment in a state of agitation and would not have been able to focus lovingly on my work with my client. Instead, by using the gratitude exercise, I arrived in a state of love.

This simple healing tool is one you can easily use at any time to help you achieve a state of inner peace. And as Irving Berlin's 1954 song lyrics suggest, counting your blessings instead of sheep is a great way to help you fall asleep at night!

TOOL 16
MAKING & USING A TREASURE MAP

*T*his is a fun and creative manifesting process that I learned from my good friend, Jan Knight. You can do it alone, or you can have a treasure mapping party with your friends where each person creates a treasure map to bring home and use.

✷ SUPPLIES NEEDED:

> » A large piece of poster board
> » Old magazines that you don't mind cutting up (or you can also search the Internet for images that are appropriate and print them out for use in your treasure map)
> » Scissors
> » Glue Stick

✷ MAKING YOUR TREASURE MAP

Begin by making a list of things you want to manifest (i.e., a new house, a new car, a peaceful world, money in the bank, etc.) Once you have your list, go through the magazines and cut out pictures and words representing items on your list. Make a check mark by each item on your list for which you have found a

are published as one volume incorporating all three books. I personally found that starting with *The Manual for Teachers* was a good way to begin. It's short and helps to get you acquainted with *The Course*.

If you are joining a study group, you will, of course, follow the format of the group in studying *The Course*. If, however, you are starting your own study group or have decided to study it on your own, you may wish to follow the advice in *The Course* which suggests repeatedly that you get in touch with your Inner Teacher. You can do this by simply holding the book in your hand, closing your eyes and asking for guidance on how to begin your study.

The Text is the theoretical foundation of *The Course* and obviously is important to read to provide a basis for the lessons in *The Workbook*. To quote from the **Introduction** of *The Workbook*: "A theoretical foundation such as the text provides is necessary as a framework to make the exercises in this workbook meaningful. Yet it is doing the exercises that will make the goal of the course possible. An untrained mind can accomplish nothing. It is the purpose of this workbook to train your mind to think along the lines the text sets forth."

From my personal experience, however, I found the ideas presented in *The Text* were more easily understood after Victor and I had completed *The Workbook*. We took a year to progress through *The Workbook* doing one lesson each day in consecutive order not worrying whether or not we "got" the lesson. We trusted we were getting it on some level and also found it became easier to understand as we progressed through the lessons.

The Workbook has 365 lessons. Some lessons are very short — only a paragraph or two. Others are longer with a few pages of text, especially when introducing new ideas. The important thing to remember in your journey through *The Workbook* is that it is not simply a book to be read — it is to be experienced. *The Workbook* often gives instructions on exercises to be done throughout the day. These exercise instructions are periodically repeated later on in *The Workbook*. All of this is geared to help you change your perception of what is real. It is an extraordinary journey!

After we completed *The Workbook*, Victor and I took turns reading to each other from *The Text* each morning during our meditation. We found that it, too, took a year to complete. Sometimes we would read several pages. Other times we would read only a paragraph, particularly if the idea presented was hard to grasp or in some cases so profound it took our breath away.

Following our reading each morning, we would go into silence for a few minutes to let what we had just read permeate our consciousness. We followed our silent time with a discussion period to explore the ideas in the reading. These discussions helped both of us understand the material at a deeper level.

Once we had completed *The Workbook* and *The Text*, we began another year with *The Workbook*. We both found it interesting to see how much more we understood it the second time around.

All of the preceding are merely suggestions. There is no right way or wrong way to study *A Course in Miracles*. Simply by having the willingness and making the commitment to pursue this self-study course, in whatever way works for you, will help you shift your perception and deepen your connection with Spirit.

We have found the study of *A Course in Miracles* to be one of our most powerful tools in helping to guide us on our path to achieving personal empowerment and inner peace.

5-CHAPTER STORY EXERCISE

*V*ictor introduced me to the 5-Chapter Story years ago. Neither of us actually knows where it originated. However, since my introduction to it, I have used it as a personal diagnostic tool to help me measure my progress through challenging situations and also to help me understand where I am at in my healing process.

I also use it with my clients to help them ascertain what "chapter" they are experiencing when they feel stuck in a repeating pattern or when they are having difficulty moving beyond a situation.

I share it here with you and I invite you to use it to identify any patterns that do not serve you and to help you see where you might be stuck in your process.

Begin by using the outline on the following page to determine what chapter you are in. Then read the description of each chapter, and the story that follows, to gain a deeper understanding of how to use this exercise as a simple healing tool.

THE 5-CHAPTER STORY

CHAPTER ONE
I was walking down the street and
I fell into this big black hole.
It was not my fault.
The hole was dark and scary
and it took me a really long time to get out.

CHAPTER TWO
I was walking down the street and
I fell into this big black hole.
It still was not my fault and it was
still dark and scary.
But the hole was familiar.
I knew how to get out
and got out quickly.

CHAPTER THREE
I was walking down the street and
I saw this big black hole.
I chose to jump in.
I got out very quickly.

CHAPTER FOUR
I was walking down the street and
I saw this big black hole.
I chose to walk around it.

CHAPTER FIVE
I walked down a different street.

❋ **Chapter One** is the situation where you feel like
a victim. Something horrible happens and you
find yourself dwelling in a black hole of despair
feeling scared and helpless with seemingly no
escape. We've all been there. When we are in
Chapter One, the first step is to recognize that
we are in a hole and ask for help in getting out.
This can be in the form of calling a trusted friend,
going to a therapist, or using prayer and meditation to call in what it is you need. The important
step here is to focus on what you want instead of
focusing on what you do not want (i.e., "I want to
be out of this hole" instead of "I don't want to be
in this hole" or "I want someone to help me out of
this hole" instead of "I'm all alone and don't have
anyone to help me out of this hole."). By focusing
on what you want, you attract the help you need.

❋ **Chapter Two** is similar to Chapter One except
you recognize that you have been in this hole
before. It is still scary but because you have been
there and gotten out before, you know that it is
possible to get out again. However, you may still
need help, so by all means, take the steps you
need to get help.

❋ **Chapter Three** is a tipping point! You can recognize when you are in Chapter Three because
the hole is so familiar you realize that you actually
chose to jump in — no one pushed you! This is
the stage when you begin to see a pattern. By recognizing you chose to jump into the hole you have
taken your first step out of victim mode and onto
the path of personal empowerment.

✳ **Chapter Four** is the most difficult to recognize. It is when you acknowledge that you have "been there, done that" and just want to jump from Chapter Three to Chapter Five, skipping over Chapter Four completely. You do not want to be faced with the temptation to jump in the hole — you just want it to go away. I have come to realize, however, that it is important we work our way through ALL FIVE chapters if we truly wish to heal a pattern in our lives. Chapter Four is the most healing chapter. It is the one where you can **see** the pattern and where you find the strength and courage to consciously **choose** to walk around it. It is where you heal your victimhood and feel true empowerment. If you choose to skip Chapter Four and go right to Chapter Five (i.e., avoiding the problem/issue instead of seeing it and recognizing that you can walk around it), then you will never completely heal the pattern.

✳ **Chapter Five** is a true release! Once you have gone through the first four chapters, the last chapter is a cakewalk. You have healed your pattern and without any effort you can now choose to embark on a new, empowering path.

The following story illustrates how to use this process to evaluate where you are in a situation and to guide you through the healing process:

Mary is in an abusive relationship with John. She feels unappreciated, disrespected and unloved. She is very unhappy in this relationship but feels powerless to end it. She is in Chapter One. She needs help to get out of the hole she is in. She gets the help she needs and breaks up with John.

Mary now goes through a series of relationships that are similar to the relationship she had with John. She is in Chapter Two. She does not understand why she keeps attracting this type of man into her life. She still feels like it is beyond her control. However, because of her past experience with John, she is able to end the relationships more quickly.

Mary begins to step out of the victim mode and do some personal growth work. She recognizes she has a pattern of attracting a certain type of man and wants to understand why. Through her personal growth work she becomes empowered and learns much about herself. During this stage, she attracts another man into her life who she knows will treat her in the same way as the others, yet she chooses to jump into the relationship. She realizes it was her decision to jump in the hole and it takes her no time to jump back out. She is now in Chapter Three.

Mary continues her personal growth work and even though she is becoming more empowered, she is still attracting the same type of man into her life. Her personal empowerment now enables her, however, to feel the attraction, recognize the pattern and consciously choose NOT to get involved. She is in Chapter Four.

Having seen the pattern for what it is and having healed her addiction to it, Mary now is ready to walk a different path – a path were she will open up to the possibilities of meeting and attracting a different type of man into her life. Mary, through her personal growth work, has become empowered. She has successfully completed all five chapters!

TOOL 19
ENGAGE YOUR ANGELS TO EXPAND TIME

*O*ften when we are faced with a large task that needs to be accomplished in a short period of time, we can become overwhelmed by its enormity. This often makes it next to impossible to get a grip on what needs to be done because our mind is in a state of anxiety.

This is a tool you can use to help quiet your mind and to get clarity on the steps needed to complete the task. If it seems that you could never get all the steps done in the allotted time, use this tool to expand time.

★ STEP 1: PREPARATION

Take the time to make a list of all the things needed to complete the task. If you are unclear about the steps needed to accomplish the task, your first step is to get clarity. You can do this by going into a meditation (see Tool 5: Meditation) and asking for clarity. Have a tablet and pen or pencil within easy reach so you can write down what comes to you in the meditation.

You can use your own prayer, or the following prayer, to begin your meditation:

Holy Spirit, I ask for clarity in completing the task that is before me. Help me to see the steps I need to take to finish the task.

Then in the silence, begin to write down what comes to you. Don't worry about writing down the steps in order. What is important is to write down everything that comes to mind about what is needed to complete the task. You can put the steps in order after you have written them down and completed your meditation.

This is an important first step, because you need to be clear about the scope of the plan before you ask your angels to assist you in expanding time.

❈ STEP 2: ENGAGING YOUR ANGELS

Now with your list before you and knowing how much time you have before the task needs to be completed, take a deep cleansing breath and say the following (or similar) prayer:

I call upon all my angels and guides to help me complete this task. I ask for your help to stay focused and energized and, if necessary, I ask that you expand time to accommodate the completion of this task. Thank you!

Now, come out of your meditative state, take a couple of deep breaths and go to work knowing that you have engaged Divine help in completing your task on time!

TOOL 20
STAYING IN THE NOW EXERCISE

*No one imagines that a symphony is supposed to
improve in quality as it goes along, or that the
whole object of playing it is to reach the finale.
The point of music is discovered in
every moment of playing and listening to it.
It is the same, I feel, with the greater part of our lives,
and if we are unduly absorbed in improving them
we may forget altogether to live them.*

~Alan Watts, Philosopher (1915-1973)

This is a simple tool to be used when you find
yourself worrying about the future or dwelling
on a disquieting event that may have happened
in the past. If you are in either of these states, you are
not experiencing the present moment. This exercise
can help bring you back into the "now" by refocusing
your attention. I like to call it, "Nowing Myself."

Close your eyes and take a few deep breaths. Bring
your attention to your body. Start noticing your bodily
sensations — your heartbeat, skin temperature, your
breath. Tighten the muscles in your legs and then relax
them, noticing how it feels. Then tighten the muscles in
your arms and relax them, again noticing how it feels.
Then move your attention to the sounds outside of
you. Notice the sounds around you — a bird chirping,

a furnace running, voices in the background, the wind rustling the trees, and so on.

Now open your eyes and look around you as you make the following statement:

> *I am here now!* *The past is past and the future is yet to come.* *I am here now!*

This short exercise will help you "*Now Yourself*," refocusing your attention and bringing you back into the present moment.

TOOL 21
LASER OF INTENT EXERCISE

*U*se this exercise when you have a clear picture of something you want to manifest in your life.

STEP 1: Go into a meditative state holding in mind a picture of the final outcome of what it is you want to manifest. For instance:

> If you have a physical condition you want to heal, focus mentally on a picture of you looking and feeling vibrant and healthy.

> If you want to sell your house, focus mentally on a picture of a buyer ringing the doorbell, coming in, looking around and saying, "I love it! I'll take it!"

> If you want to raise money, focus mentally on a picture of going to your mailbox everyday and finding lots of envelopes filled with money, or mentally see a picture of your bank statement indicating that you have lots of money in your account.

❈ STEP 2: Hold your vision for three to five minutes, actually seeing your vision already manifested as a reality.

❈ STEP 3: Come out of your meditative state and notice the happiness and gratitude you feel.

❈ STEP 4: Strive to keep yourself in a state of gratitude. Throughout the day, whenever you find yourself slipping into a state of discouragement or fear or lack, bring to mind your vision of having already manifested your desire. At these times, you can also use the Free Yourself from Fear process to transform all limiting thoughts you may have and get yourself back into the gratitude of manifestation!

Practice this exercise each day, along with the other manifestation tools listed below until you have manifested what it is you want to attract into your life.

» Tool 9: Free Yourself from Fear Process (p. 181)
» Tool 14: Law of Attraction Exercise (p. 193)
» Tool 16: Making & Using a Treasure Map (p. 199)

TOOL 22

THE TRUTHFULNESS VOW

We vow to always be truthful with one another.
If one of us is feeling upset, we vow to take the time
needed to process our emotions and
bring our relationship into a state
of harmony and balance.
~ *Carol Hansen & Victor Grey*

This tool, I feel, is right at the top of the list when it comes to creating a balanced, healthy and loving relationship of trust between two indi-viduals. If one of the parties in the relationship is upset and keeps that feeling inside, the energy between the two becomes strained and the original upset, which may have been minor, begins to consume more and more energy, throwing the relationship out of balance.

In order for a truthfulness vow to be effective, some ground rules need to be established and agreed upon by both parties. Following is a process Victor and I have used successfully. The time it takes will vary depending on the size of the issue. However we have noticed, the more we use the process the easier it becomes for us to reach resolution and return to a harmonious state.

❧ THE TRUTHFULNESS AGREEMENT PROCESS

❧ 1. *We both agree*: when either of us is feeling upset by something that has happened in our relationship, we will give ourselves time to get in touch with our emotions and to think through the reasons for our upset.

❧ 2. *We both agree:* that once we have gotten clear about the reasons for our upset (i.e., identifying the thoughts fueling the emotion), we will set aside adequate time for the two of us to talk and process our emotions.

❧ 3. *We both agree:* to hold a space of safety during our processing time for each of us to express our feelings without interruption. We will listen from the heart, earnestly making an effort to put ourselves in the other person's shoes.

❧ 4. *We both agree:* to take responsibility for our own feelings and to express how we are feeling without blaming the other for causing our upset.

(For example, the upset person may begin with: "When I expect you home at a certain time and you're late without calling me, I get worried that you may have been in an accident. It's important to me that you call me when you are going to be late.") In this example the listening person is told of the expectation *(i.e., that the listener will be home at a certain time)*, of the upset person's feeling when that expectation is not met *(I get worried)*

and what the upset person wants in the future *(a phone call)*. By comparison, a blaming statement might go something like this: *"I'm really angry because you never let me know when you are going to be late. It's so irresponsible of you not to let me know!"*

✴ 5. **We both agree:** to mirror back to the each other what we have heard, asking if that is correct, to ensure there is no misunderstanding in communication between us.

   (In this instance, the listener would say to the upset person, "What I hear you say is that you were scared when I didn't call to let you know I was going to be late and from now on you would like me to make sure I call you when I'm not going to home on time. Is that correct?")

✴ 6. **We both agree:** once the upset has been stated, mirrored back and understood, the listening person will say, *"Tell me more."*
   This gives the upset person more opportunity to fully express any other thoughts that are fueling the upset.

✴ 7. **We both agree:** if other thoughts come up, we will continue to repeat steps 5 and 6 until all thoughts fueling the upset have been expressed and acknowledged.

✴ 8. **We both agree:** once the upset person feels complete, the roles will be reversed giving the listening person an opportunity to express his/her thoughts that might be fueling any emotions he/she is feeling.

(For example: "I felt so stressed at work today that I needed to unwind before I came home. I understand now that it's important for me to call so you don't worry. It's also important to me to know, when I come home after a stressful day I will be able to take 15 to 30 minutes of quiet time by myself just to unwind.)

(Repeat steps 5, 6 and 7.)

* 9. *We both agree:* once the process feels complete, we will reach an agreement on how to move forward.

Complete the process with a prayer of gratitude, similar to the one below, for the loving relationship of trust that you are building together.

We give thanks for this opportunity to deepen our relationship of trust and to grow our love for one another.

TOOL 23
KARMIC DEBT RELEASE PROCESS

*T*his tool is adapted from a process described by friend and author, John English in his novel, *The Shift: An Awakening*. The process I share here is a shortened version you can easily use to release karmic debts owed to you, thus freeing yourself from the "ties that bind" you to painful events and people from your past.

You may believe it is important to hold on to the memories of these painful events, thinking the memories will act as a shield protecting you from being victimized again. This, however, is a false perception. Rather than protecting you, such memories keep you in a state of separation and disempowerment. In such a state, it is impossible to reach a place of harmony and inner peace — the true path to personal empowerment.

The following process is a powerful form of forgiveness. It is one of several tools described in this book to help you overcome this particular obstacle blocking your path to personal empowerment and inner peace. The other tools recommended are listed at the end of this chapter.

❦ KARMIC DEBT RELEASE PROCESS

❦ **STEP 1:** Go into a quiet space and take a few deep cleansing breaths, feeling your body relax more and more with each breath.

❦ **STEP 2:** Putting your hand over your heart, think of the person who has wronged you.

❦ **STEP 3:** Say the following prayer out loud *(substituting "Holy Spirit" with whatever Divine Being you are comfortable working with)*:

> *Holy Spirit, my desire is to reach a state*
> *of harmony, love and inner peace.*
> *With you as my witness,*
> *I hereby release all karmic debt owed me:*
> *past, present and future — for all time!*
> *I release it NOW!*

❦ **STEP 4:** Take another deep, cleansing breath and feel the release!

❦ **STEP 5:** Express your gratitude by saying the following (or similar) prayer

> *Holy Spirit, I am truly grateful for the freedom I now feel*
> *and I thank you for being my witness during*
> *this healing experience.*

Note: For this tool to be a truly effective healing and empowering experience, I suggest that you use any one or all of the following processes prior to using this tool:

- » Kything Meditation (Tool 5, p. 165)
- » Free Yourself from Fear Process (Tool 9, p. 181)
- » Emotional Release Exercise (Tool 12, p. 189)
- » Mirror Exercise (Tool 13, p. 191)

TOOL 24
NEW YEAR'S JOURNAL PROCESS

*V*ictor and I do this process every New Year's Eve. It can be done alone, with a spouse or partner, or as a family ritual. There are no specific "rules" for doing it right. The point is to set aside time each year to write down everything of importance that has happened during the past year and your goals for the coming year.

What you need:

* ☙ A bound journal or spiral notebook
* ☙ A pen or pencil
* ☙ A quiet space where you can be undisturbed

We always begin our process with a short prayer asking our angels to help us remember all the events that were important to us during the past year.

Start your journal by dating the first page so you know the year you began the journal. You can use the same journal every year until it is filled. If you decide to use the same journal each year, be sure to leave a few blank pages between each year's entries so you can add items later you may have forgotten to add during the process.

The following is a starter list of activities and experiences you might want to document in your journal. (Be sure to add any other topic to this list that is important to you). Title each page with the topic you are covering and always leave a couple of blank pages between each topic to allow space to add things that come to mind later.

* **Family Events** (births, deaths, family reunions, meaningful family experiences, etc.)
* **New People** (all the people you have met during the past year and how they made a difference in your life)
* **Trips** (all the trips and vacations you have taken and what was special about each one)
* **Activities and Events** (all the creative endeavors you have engaged in over the past year and events you have attended and why each was meaningful)
* **Accomplishments** (all the things you have accomplished throughout the year and why these things were important to you)

After Victor and I finish our list, we look at the goals we had written in our journal for the past year and check off those we have accomplished. We then write our goals for the coming year, carrying over any goals from last year that were not yet accomplished or remain unfinished and are still relevant.

When we complete our journal entries, we end with a short prayer of gratitude for the past year and ask for guidance to accomplish the goals we have set forth for the new year.

TOOL 25
ANONYMOUS DO-GOODER
DAILY RITUAL

*I have never been especially impressed by the heroics of people
convinced that they are about to change the world.
I am more awed by those who struggle to make
one small difference after another.*

~ *Ellen Goodman, Author & Columnist*

*T*his is a tool I learned about many years ago. It has
a double bonus: it makes me feel good and at the
same time adds positive energy to the planet.

The ritual itself is very easy. Simply commit to doing
some good deed or act of kindness every day — anonymously. This could involve picking up a piece of litter
and disposing of it properly, saying a kind word to a
clerk in a store, smiling at a stranger, paying a bridge toll
for the car behind you, throwing back a tennis ball that
has gone over the fence, slowing down to let a car into
traffic ahead of you, and so on.

The world abounds with opportunities to do good
deeds. The movie, *Pay It Forward*, is a great story of
how simple good deeds can multiply and create a positive change in energy. If everyone committed to doing
an anonymous good deed every day with no expectation

of getting something in return, I believe it would create a positive shift in the planet toward love and good will.

TOOL 26

PRAYERS

Following are prayers I have specifically mentioned in this book. Feel free to adapt them using your own words and substituting "Holy Spirit" with whatever Divine Being you are comfortable using in the prayer. These prayers are offered simply as a guide. The ending prayer in any exercise is a simple prayer of thanksgiving.

FREE YOURSELF FROM FEAR PRAYERS:

"Holy Spirit, shine your light of truth on this situation. Enable me to identify and turn over to you for transformation all the limiting thoughts keeping me from achieving a state of inner peace and being my full expression of love."

"Holy Spirit, I ask to be released from this feeling of anger. Shine your light of truth on my relationship with [insert name here]. Dispel all my illusions and bring me to a state of peace."

FINDING THE GIFT PRAYER:

"Holy Spirit, shine your light of truth on this situation. Help me to see the bigger picture and understand the gift being given to me. Dispel all my illusions and bring me to a state of peace."

⚜ RELATIONSHIP PRAYER OF THANKSGIVING:

"We give thanks for this opportunity to deepen our relationship of trust and to grow in our love for one another."

⚜ MIRROR EXERCISE PRAYER:

"Holy Spirit, shine your light of truth on my relationship with [insert name]. Show me how this relationship serves as a mirror revealing areas within myself in need of healing. Help me to heal those areas and to reach a state of inner peace. "

⚜ EXPANDING TIME PRAYERS:

"Holy Spirit, I ask for clarity in completing the task before me. Help me to see the steps needed to finish the task."

"I call upon all my angels and guides to help me complete the task before me. I ask you to help me stay focused and energized and to expand time, if necessary, to accommodate the completion of this task. Thank you!"

⚜ KARMIC DEBT RELEASE PRAYER:

"Holy Spirit, my desire is to reach a state of harmony, love and inner peace. With you as my witness, I hereby release all karmic debt owed me: past, present and future — for all time! I release it NOW!"

✤ ENDING PRAYERS OF THANKSGIVING:

"Holy Spirit, thank you for being my partner in this sacred, healing work."

"Holy Spirit, I am truly grateful for the freedom I now feel and I thank you for being my witness during this healing experience."

Part 3

The Resources

STARTER LIST OF RESOURCES

This section contains a beginning list of resources that can help get you started on your healing journey. A more extensive list can be found on the SimpleHealingTools.com website under the Resources section. New resources are being continually added to the website, so check it often.

MEDITATION PRODUCTS

- Dancing Helix (www.dancinghelix.com) We use this in our meditation room as a wonderful way to focus our attention as we begin our daily meditations.

- Tibetan Bowls (available from local metaphysical bookstores and online)

- Crystals (available from local metaphysical bookstores and online)

INFORMATION

- World Peace Flame Candles (WorldPeaceFlame.org)

- World Peace Experiment (onlyloveprevails.org)

- Database of A Course in Miracles Study Groups (miraclecenter.org/services/study_groups.html)

❈ ONLINE SERVICES

- ❈ Totally Unique Thoughts: Short, Empowering Daily Email Messages (www.tut.com)

- ❈ Daily Law of Attraction Quotes Emailed to you (www.abraham-hicks.com)

❈ BOOKS & CDS

- ❈ *Lighten Up Inspirations Workbook* and CD (openheartpress.com)

- ❈ *Free Yourself from Fear* CD and Booklet (openheartpress.com)

- ❈ A Course in Miracles (books and CDs) (shop.acim.org)

- ❈ *Law of Attraction* books and CDs by Abraham Hicks (abraham-hicks.com)

- ❈ *Law of Attraction: The Science of Attracting More of What you Want and Less of What you Don't* by Michael Losier (LawOfAttractionBook.com)

- ❈ Essene Book of Days from the Earth Stewards Network (earthstewards.org)

❈ WEBSITES

- ❈ SimpleHealingTools.com

- ❈ OnlyLovePrevails.org

- ❈ OpenHeart.com

- ❈ OpenHeartPress.com

- ❈ ACIM.org (official site of the Foundation for Inner Peace, original publishers of A Course in Miracles)

CPSIA information can be obtained
at www.ICGtesting.com
Printed in the USA
LVOW11s0852130517

534408LV00001B/115/P